ON THE MOORS OF OMAHA

Essays

Also by Trebbe Johnson

Fierce Consciousness: Surviving the Sorrows of Earth and Self

Radical Joy for Hard Times: Finding Meaning and Making Beauty in Earth's Broken Places

You've Made the Earth More Beautiful!

101 Ways to Make Guerrilla Beauty

The World Is a Waiting Lover: Desire and the Quest for the Beloved

For Lonnie Hansen Pierson Dunbier
In gratitude for recognizing the writer
in my awkward, yearning 15-year-old self

AUTHOR'S NOTE

Most of these essays, some in slightly different forms, have been previously published: "Where's the Temple," "Devoting," "Kissed by Fire," and "Lament and Praise for the Earth" in *Parabola*; "Witness to a Landscape" in *Prism*; "Yards" in *Boulevard;* "The Coal Remembers" in the anthology *Kinship: Practice*; "On the Moors of Omaha" in *Fine Lines*; "The Juniper Tree" in *Kosmos*; "Travel in a Dangerous County" in the anthology *Kinship with the Animals*; "Drought" in *Blue Mesa Review*; "Caring for the Waste" in *New Age Journal*; and "Gaze Even Here," "Uncommon Gratitude," and "11 Interventions in the 10 Days of Your Dying" in *Orion*.

CONTENTS

PROLOGUE

Here's how I think of an essay.

It's like a poem, in that it explores a certain moment, object, or idea without coming right out and declaring what that provocation was.

Unlike a poem, however, it shares its pathways of exploration in complete sentences, without line breaks. It doesn't make you ponder and reread as much as a good poem does. You can relax, muse, flow.

An essay is like a hike on which certain features show up with enough regularity that you begin to pay attention to them. For example, say you're on a long walk that takes you through both countryside and small villages, and you realize that indigo flowers keep appearing — growing wild in meadows, pushing up in the crack of a sidewalk, planted in a pot on a front porch. You start looking for indigo flowers.

An essay mixes fact and experience. It's nonfiction, like journalism, but nonfiction with a decisively personal point of view. It's Author-in-the-World. Readers can't look into your brain and fact-check you, but if they could, they would be reassured to know that you have told the truth.

I first encountered the essay form when I was a sophomore in high school, and our English teacher, Miss Hansen, assigned one for us to write every week. It was writing those papers and receiving the guidance and praise of my teacher that convinced me I really could be the writer I had dreamed of being. I describe Miss Hansen, those essays, and my creative awakening in the essay for which this book is named.

It wasn't until the early 1980s, however, that I really began to delve into the essay as a particularly engaging form of reading and writing. That happened when I discovered *Orion* Magazine, founded in 1982. The intricately wrought, nature-themed essays they published in each issue prompted me to seek out other essayists, like Annie Dillard, Gretel Ehrlich, Scott Russell Sanders, E.B. White, Joan Didion Wendell Berry, and Barry Lopez. Moving back in time, I read Kenko, Michel de Montaigne, William Hazlitt, and Virginia Woolf. Ralph Waldo Emerson was a favorite; I loved the excess of his lyricism. I studied what these writers did and tried to glean pointers on how to write essays of my own.

My first essay, published in 1984 and included here, was "Witness to a Landscape," about a moment of revelation I experienced on a frosty morning in England's Berkshire Downs, where I was living at the time. For years I submitted essays to *Orion*, and for years they were rejected until, finally, they were not. I wrote my first essay for *Parabola* in 1988, when that estimable magazine of myth and tradition was fourteen years old, and, after many more on many themes, my last one in 2024, just before *Parabola* ceased publication in the spring of 2025. The other essays in this book were published in several literary magazines.

I continue to love essays. Some essayists, like Zadie Smith, Linda Hogan, and (still) Dillard and Emerson, can provoke in me that writerly squall of responses that is both awe of the mastery and envy that I didn't write the piece myself. For me, an essay usually begins with a couple of scraps of fascination that I suspect may be connected in some way I cannot fathom. I start writing and eventually, usually after several drafts, the essay itself begins to tell me what it's about.

My husband, Andy Gardner, used to urge me to publish a book of my essays, and finally, five years after his death, I am taking his advice. These pieces say a great deal about who I am, what I have cared about, and how I've muddled and punched through hard times. Mostly, they reveal how it's possible to be graced and changed by the teachers who show up unexpectedly in life — for a year or moment, as a stranger on a subway platform, a wave of incoming tide, or a ravaged forest. The world is constantly extending invitations to us to pause for a moment and take in what one of these ephemeral teachers has to offer, and through these essays I spotlight them.

PART I
Apprentice To The Land

WHERE'S THE TEMPLE?

When I was in my mid-twenties, a garden at twilight told me a secret. This garden taught me how to see the wondrous amidst its camouflage, and the lesson has guided me ever since.

I had moved on that midsummer day into an old stone cottage in the Berkshire Downs of England. I fell in love with the cottage the minute I saw it. It was an old farming cottage in a tiny village of about 150 people, and it faced the downs, those hills that ripple out endlessly under the sky. Not far away was the famous Uffington White Horse, a stylized horse carved into the chalk on a hillside a thousand years before. Before I even went inside the cottage, I loved it for the garden — a tangled, overgrown, wild patch that ran all the way from the road up to the gabled door. Lilies, roses, daisies, and bachelor buttons bloomed extravagantly. It reminded me of *The Secret Garden*, a book I had loved as a child. I had always hoped to stumble upon a secret garden, and this seemed to be it.

A few days later I moved in. I hoped to live frugally enough so I could stay for a year, devoting my time to writing. I wanted to get things off to a good start, so that very night I started setting up my desk in the upstairs room, which would also be my bedroom. I was standing before the open casement windows that overlooked the garden and creating a desk for myself out of an old wooden door and two sturdy crates. It was late, after 9 o'clock. The June nights come on slowly that far north, and the downs were finally settling into shadow, although certain details of the village street and the garden remained discernible.

Then, at the periphery of my attention, something glowed. I looked up from my adjustments on the desk to see what it was. A patch of lilies, which had been white as starlight in the day, now flared silver in the bluing twilight. All the plants in the garden had faded to dark except those lilies, which looked at that moment, as if they were radiating back into the oncoming night some of the sun they had absorbed by day. And then, as I marveled at this botanical perseverance, the lilies were extinguished. The color simply faded and all the garden was plunged into night.

I was stunned. It was as if I had peered into a cosmic process humans are rarely given to see. I had glanced through a crack in a door and beheld an exalted place — the ordinary yet highly secretive adjustments that Nature patterns and manipulates to work life on Earth. If I had looked up just seconds earlier or seconds later, I would not have been privy to the sight of lilies holding the last light of day and would not have seen that light drain out of them.

And in that instant I understood that if I were to pay attention to the spaces between and just behind the things I *thought* I needed to look at, there was no limit to what I might witness.

There is a doorway into the world beyond the known. At least that's what I believed as a child. I was always on the lookout for it — glancing sideways at nesting birds, climbing trees and pretending I lived there, cracking the ice on ponds and puddles, staring at one spot in the sky. It's human to wish to probe the mystery, not just as children but all our lives and in many ways. We long to peer into the remote and inaccessible, because we imagine those elusive places to be more exalted than the common areas we pass through easily. They seem to hold a truth that, because it is unknown, must therefore be lofty and magnificent and, once tapped, will be part of us as well. The mountain climber drawn to high peaks, the Lakota seekers who fast alone for four days and nights to receive a vision, the poet seeking a more revealing description of reality, the scientist who explores the micro- and macro-universes, and all who question, practice, probe for the path they'll know only when they step onto it — all are on similar searches. They aspire to perceive the unknown world more clearly and experience it more intimately. Humans are endowed with what Jung called "divine curiosity," which "yearns to be born and does not shrink from conflict, suffering, or sin." Jung was talking about consciousness here, about how hauling the unconscious into the bright air of consciousness sates this divine curiosity. But you could say that we are all seized to a greater or lesser degree by a divine curiosity that makes us feel we're just on the verge of perceiving the one thing that will clarify and even redeem everything else.

Yet in the secret world, the keepers of the mystery, whether birds, gods, oil paint, supernovas, or wilderness, are often loath to share their secrets with us mortal curious. Myth, legend, and lore remind us of this truth over and over. When Actaeon spied the goddess Artemis at her bath, she punished him by turning him into a stag, and his own hunting dogs tore him to bits. Psyche lost her beloved Eros when she shone a light on him after a night of passion, something she had promised never to do. When Bluebeard's wife peeked into the room that her husband had forbidden her to enter, she marked herself as the next corpse fated to be stowed there. And everyone knows that a person who finds his or her way into the realm of fairy and later leaves, either by escape or permission, will instantly age a hundred years upon returning to the world he assumed he'd left behind just days before. These and other audacious humans and their terrible fates are cited by the cautious as proof that those who peer into what is forbidden, invisible, and impenetrable will be punished. Galileo, at point of torture, was forced to recant his findings that the Earth moves around the sun. The masterpiece, "Death of the Virgin," by the Renaissance painter Caravaggio, was condemned for "realism bordering on blasphemy." Even today scientists exploring stem cell medicine and genetics are thought to be encroaching on fields best left to God.

If the gods do permit a human a glimpse of the sublime, it can be too much. In the *Mahabharata*, when Arjuna begs to see Krishna in his divine form, the god consents. But he warns Arjuna that he is going to provide him with a "divine eye," since no human could withstand an unmitigated view of such splendor. Even equipped with this special aid, Arjuna is terrified by the vision that appears before him. Yet how does he respond? Does he turn away? Does he beg for mercy? No, he longs for more!

> Tell me —
> who are you
> in this terrible form?
> Homage to you, Best of Gods!
> I want to know you
> as you are in your beginning.

I thought of Arjuna, dashed and sizzling after being granted the vision he so longed for, when I read about the epiphany of the self-trained nineteenth-century scholar George Smith. Smith was in the British Museum poring over ancient clay tablets that had been discovered in what is now Iran and that were covered with an unknown writing. Suddenly the fog parted and Smith understood with absolute certainty that what he was reading was a tale of the Flood. He was so excited by his discovery that he leaped up from the table and started tearing off his clothes. And then, after he had calmed down a bit, he returned to his work and continued to penetrate the text that, thanks to him, was soon to become known to the world as *The Epic of Gilgamesh.*

It's not just the genius or the personal friend of a god who can be privy to great visions. All it takes, really, is patience and looking just on the periphery of the obvious. Seeing the lilies in the garden extinguish the light of day was a boon, especially since the revelation happened on my very first night there. Beginning the next morning, I took walks every day in the woods, hills, and fields, and then I'd stop walking and simply wait and look. My goal was to wait patiently until something amazing happened, and eventually, invariably, it did. The reflection of a hawk flew over a pond. The wind chased the light across the field. A red fox dashed through the snow. Walking through a field in a thick fog, I heard the sounds of invisible cows munching all around me. The moon turned the village church silver. A single red berry twirled crazily on the end of a vine. This way of seeing accompanied me throughout that year in England and during several dark years back in New York, and it has informed the work I do, which stems from exploring how simple and profound it is to spend time in nature, both wild and wounded, and pay attention to what arises within and without.

I have never forgotten the lesson of the lilies, for it is valid everywhere, and not just in nature either. I have been granted access to amazement in a subway, a recycling center, a plane, even a funeral home. As John Berger, who has widely explored the avenues of seeing, has written: "Not to say that *behind* appearances is the truth, the Platonic way. It is very possible that visibility *is* the truth and that what lies outside visibility are only the 'traces' of what has been or will become visible."

Japanese designers build the interplay of the visible and invisible into the gardens they create. The aesthetic principle of *miegakure*, or "hide and reveal," celebrates the ever-shifting delights of overlapping perspective along the path that meanders through the garden, so that only a slim glimpse of rock, tree, koi swimming in pond, or waterfall is visible at any one time. It is said that *miegakure* imparts vastness to a small space. Like newly formed neuronal pathways in the brain, the garden path constantly presents the visitor with impressions that arise afresh and in unfamiliar relationships to other impressions. All the way along, something is a little bit hidden and is a little bit revealed. You never know what vision, what insight will emerge, and from where.

When we see, the world *enters* us through neuronal pathways. And contrary to what we may assume, it does not flow from eyes to brain as a stream of purely objective data. We build the gates that receive our world and can rebuild them at any time. The neuronal pathways that inform how and what we see are plastic, and they change and adapt not just when we're young but throughout our lives. When neurons that are highly connected, or "facilitated," are repeatedly stimulated, they require relatively little input to fire and so pass the signal of recognition on to the next neuron and so on, ever deeper into the network. Laura Sewall, ecologist and author of *Sight and Sensibility*, writes that, like fish swimming through rocks in the sea, the pattern of firing wants to take the path of least resistance. We see what we're used to seeing, what we expect to see. However, vision can change. "Plasticity is not simply a matter of developmental phrase. More essentially, it's the act of attending (the amount of 'arousal') in traditional neurophysical terms) that makes the critical difference. It is being as excited as a child and as mindful as an adult that makes all the difference." In order to see the unfamiliar, the beckoning, the truly revelatory, we need to open up new pathways for those neurons. We need to look between the lines, nod to the obvious, and then glance quickly to the side where the not-so-obvious resides.

The Lakota holy man Black Elk taught the spiritual version of this scientific truth. Speaking about *hanblecheyapi*, the ceremony of crying for a vision, he emphasized that the person who fasts in the wilderness in hopes of receiving guidance from the sacred world "must be alert to any messenger that the Great Spirit may send to him, for these people often come in the form of an animal, even one as small and as seemingly insignificant as a little ant." In other words, don't get so fixated on what you want to see or what's easy to see that you miss what's right before you and doing its best to get your attention.

The old tales remind us subtly yet repeatedly of the importance of turning our full gaze to those impressions that dance at the periphery. So many stories are about the quest, of course, the search for that one hidden treasure that will once again bring harmony to the world. But the heroines and heroes who are open to the unexpected along the way and respond appropriately to it are far more likely to succeed than the ones who see only what they've determined is worthy of their attention and reject everything else. The person who pauses to give water to an old woman or delays a critical journey in order to help an animal is the one we admire and root for. He's the one who bears a sensitivity to the whole world; she's the one who insists that there is always time to veer off course when something vital beckons. Beauty and epiphany bide their time in the sidewise glance.

On a gray, rainy afternoon on the island of Bali, a place I visit every year, I impulsively asked my driver, Eka Merta Sedana, to take me to Tanah Lot. I had never been to this temple on the sea, only accessible at low tide, for it is known to be inundated with tourists who come to take photos of the sun as it sets dramatically behind the open-sided temple. But I was curious and needed a lift. I was feeling sad because a Balinese friend was very ill and I didn't know if I'd ever see him again; because, just two weeks earlier, the devastating earthquake, tsunami, and nuclear meltdown had struck Japan and the situation was so sad and frightening; and also because, as so many people in Bali were remarking, the weather, for the third year in a row, was so unusually rainy that the flowers of the fruits and crops were being knocked off the plants, threatening the harvest. Why not stop at Tanah Lot?

The parking lot was huge, and the long, narrow street between it and the temple was crammed on both sides with tiny stalls selling T-shirts, food, CDs, Balinese offerings, and souvenir kitsch. So far the place was meeting my low expectations. I reached the end of the street and walked down the wide stone steps that led down to large flat rocks extending into the sea. The tide was coming in. I could see at a glance that the temple, perched on a high crag perhaps a quarter mile out across the flattish, black rocks, was inaccessible. Still people from many places — Java, Japan, Australia, France, Bali, America — were trying to get as close as they could. They were wading out on the rocks to get a photo of the temple, which really did look dramatic even under the leaden skies, and to take pictures of one another with the temple or the sea in the background.

I was wandering among them, watching my footing on the rocks and thinking I wouldn't stay long, when a wave dashed in and splashed everyone. And it was in that moment of practically unanimous reaction that I saw the real spectacle in this event. Every time a wave washed over the rocks and dowsed the crowd, people burst into shrieks of delighted laughter. They were acknowledging this moment of happiness, moreover, not just among their own friends, but with whomever was nearby. It was a shared experience. Each shower of surf against skirts, shorts, jeans, jilbabs, sarongs, and bare legs brought people's gazes together in a joyous release of national differences and personal cares. I took the lens cap off my camera and started shooting pictures.

When I re-entered the parking lot, Eka was waiting for me. I was so exhilarated that I could not stop babbling to him about what I had seen. Back in the car, I pushed the View button on my camera and showed him some of the photos I had just taken. He looked a while in silence. Then he turned to me. "Where temple?" he asked in surprise.

It was true. I had not taken one picture of the temple. For this pilgrimage had led to something more wonderful than that sacred place: it had revealed people of many lands playing together in the waves at a sacred place. Glancing just behind the foreground, I had been given to spy a wonder.

WITNESS TO A LANDSCAPE

In advanced physics there's a way of looking at the world called Heisenberg's Uncertainty Principle. It says, in effect, that any measurable subatomic process is directly influenced by the person doing the measuring. This does not mean that someone's cheating. Rather, it implies a partnership with the event.

Within the quantum landscape a subatomic particle can behave in one of two different ways: as a particle or as a wave, but it can't do both at once. The dance it does at any given moment depends on who's calling the tune. The physicist who brings wave questions and wave-measuring tools to the experiment will see a wave. The particle-watcher will see a particle. How the subatomic world is watched sways the way it manifests itself. The watcher is a participant in the event.

For a year I lived alone in an old stone cottage in a tiny village in the Berkshire Downs of England. I wrote poetry there, and read, shared tea and gossip and garden flowers with my neighbors, and was employed for a while as the village street sweeper. Most important, I learned how to become a participant in the event.

In England I learned how to watch. I watched from the inside and from the outside. From my desk on the second floor of my Pear Tree Cottage, I could look between the leaded panes of my window and frame details of the landscape beyond: a small farm with chicken coops, swatches of field, a lone chestnut tree, a bristle of woods, the downs.

I also watched from the outside. I trekked through the woods and fields, then spent long moments sitting still in one spot looking and listening, waiting in faith for exceptional events to reveal themselves.

And they did, they always did. They occurred as brief moments, gently, but with utter clarity, and each moment expressed a singular truth about its landscape.

There was the moment, for instance, when when a hawk soared through a pool of sky in the midst of the woods...

...the moment the wind blew green spring light across the field...

...the moment a flock of plovers launched from a misty slope and told the reason why in a hieroglyph of wings...

...the moment a scattering of haystacks was sanctified by moonlight...

... and the moment when, on an emptied wooden farm wagon, one cabbage leaf cupped sunset in a puddle of rainwater.

Each of these moments stood forth to declare its place in the world. Each was distinguished within its environment, the way a certain leaf or stone or twig is encapsulated and clarified under a crystalline lens of ice in a frosty field.

I must suppose the landscape could have abided without me. I must suppose it would have turned hot and cold, day and night, foggy and clear if I had not been around, and that all these small details would have kept on doing what they had to do to stitch a place for themselves in their habitat.

But I don't really believe that. I think that, like the physicist, I had to be there. It is perfectly plain to me that if I had not been paying attention, or even if I had been paying attention from a slightly different angle, that hawk would not have flown across that patch of liquid sky. I might have seen the bird in the sky, and I might have seen the pool on the ground, but I would never have witnessed the astonishing link between the two.

"The secret of the world," wrote Emerson, "is the tie between person and event."

We are the makers of the Earth's experiment.

The truth of that principle was revealed to me one frosty February morning when I caught my landscape unawares and saw that it had reserved a place for me. I had gotten up early and gone outside to watch the sun rise. I had often watched it rise from the vantage point of my desk window, so I knew its route and its schedule well, but that day I felt like being present.

The village was just beginning to thaw into its dawn awakening. Wood smoke wafted from chimneys, moving presences I could smell but not see. Lighted windows warmed a couple of houses, but all the animals and most birds were still asleep. Crunching night and silence beneath my boots, I climbed a hill that overlooked the village, and there I stood, with faith and patience as my measuring instruments, and waited for the sun to show. It took a long time, and I grew as sheer and frail as the ragged, windswept clouds, but when it finally happened, I was quite unprepared.

The sun rose in the woods. This should not have been startling, for the woods were behind the church and, as far as I had ever been able to tell from my desk, the sun these days rose from behind the church. This was different, though. This sun rose not from behind the woods, or beyond them, but in them. And I, momentarily dazzled, was convinced that the sun was actually pulsing like a great red heart within that fragile web of trees.

At that moment no logic or science could have made me disbelieve that a day was being born in my village woods. And I figured if I ran I might be able to touch it.

By the time I rounded the road that hemmed old Mick Lawler's garden, the illusion had shifted. Whether you're merely looking or whether you're trying to reach out and touch, cosmic events like to surprise; they flare in a time span bracketed only by a couple of winks. So I saw that the sun was coming up the way it usually did, and I saw that I couldn't touch it.

But the magic had been sparked and the landscape was ripe with possibilities for great events, so I veered into the field behind Mick's garden and headed toward the downs.

The grass was brushed with luminous frost, and I could look back to see the line of my footsteps cast in silver. The sky was lightening, testing its colors and remixing them, warming and fattening the ragged clouds. Up ahead, the fields were racing exuberantly toward the downs. They glowed. Green-gold they glowed, as if, in their awakening, they had learned how to produce their very own light. Then the sun burst out from behind the church; the grasses exulted; the fields redoubled their golden race. And the lone chestnut tree I had so often framed in miniature within my window pane was the pivot round which the whole morning spun. I went to stand by the chestnut tree, and then I turned around to watch.

There was my landscape, and it was waiting for me. I saw my cottage woven against a backdrop of pasture and trees, and I saw that the pasture and trees were woven into the village. The picture was intricate, perfectly detailed. I saw the chicken coops. I saw the woods where once I had witnessed the flight of a hawk through a pool. I saw that now the woods burned with light. And I saw that the footprints that had marked my passage from moments ago to now were already dissolving into the earth.

My vision was shaken. It was as if I had spent three seasons peering through a telescope that had just been lifted out of my hands, flipped around, and handed back.

I could not stare hard enough at what was happening to my cottage. There it was: the stones, the pear tree, the tangled garden, the gable over the front door, the windows. All there in their proper places, as they were meant to be. And so was the window at which I'd so often sat to frame landscapes and watch the sun rise.

The lens of the telescope clarified even more. Suddenly the view I saw became so clear it seemed in danger of fracturing.

For as I looked at that one window, I was overwhelmed by its emptiness. I was not framing landscapes at the moment, because I was in the landscape. I was a part of the field I watched. And if, at that moment, I had not been in the field, I would have been at the window, looking out across the exultant fields at the chestnut tree, marveling how it managed to stand upright on a plane of surging light.

Like my cottage at sunrise, Heisenberg's Uncertainty Principle can be viewed through a two-way telescope. Through one end I understand that what the event is depends on how I observe it. Through the other end I see that for every event I witness there will be another I must overlook. The physicist who measures the mass of a subatomic particle can't determine its motion; the one who clocks the motion misses the mass.

Or, on the visible, tangible, human scale, if I go into the woods on a quest for wildflowers, I can't devote my full attention to what the birds have to say. That's part of the uncertainty. The other part is the inevitable surprise of the event I do get a chance to watch.

I have been living back in America now for many years. When I think of my landscape beneath the Berkshire Downs, I must assume the wind is still blowing the light across the fields. I must also assume that there exist in the world other landscapes that are withholding certain conjunctions of sunlight, trees, birds, and water until I am present to witness them. For now, I do what I can to put myself in the path of the world's revelations and, when they show themselves, to open myself up to what they offer, like a cottage window framing amazement from both directions.

YARDS

There was a story my father used to tell about how I once tried to reach him over a backyard. It was in Indianapolis and he was out there one warm evening doing some work on the lawn when he heard me call out, "Hi, Daddy!" He looked up and saw me gripping the rim of my crib as I peered at him through my bedroom window. Every time he told that story, my father would mimic, very lovingly, the little child's voice, drawing long on the syllables, as I had apparently done: "Hiiii, Daa-deee." After my parents divorced, he always told it on the rare occasions we saw each other. When he got drunk, he would repeat it several times, slurringly drawing out those syllables as if, by sympathetic magic, he could induce me to call to him again, to seek him out across an expanse much more perilous than a suburban backyard in evening.

Backyards were my landscape. They made my world view as the prairie shaped Laura Ingalls Wilder and a secret garden inspirited Mary, Colin and Dicken. I lived in half a dozen of them until the age of twelve — in Indianapolis, Springfield, Illinois and Omaha. My mother had grown up in the cities of Hartford, Connecticut and New York; my father was a farm boy from east Texas. They were newlyweds in 1946, when Aetna Insurance transferred them west, and they decided to settle in the suburbs, a terrain neither had ever known. Millions of others of their generation had the same idea. After their triumph in World War II, the white American middle class was ready to reward itself. The West had been won two generations past, the frontiers pushed back as far as they would go. Trailblazers still, Americans responded to the horizon crisis by going forth to claim a parcel of the country for their own. Between 1950 and 1970, the number of Americans who lived in the suburbs doubled from 36 to 74 million. Eighty-three percent of the nation's growth during that time took place in the limbic land between city and farm.

A house in the suburbs was the post-war ticket to true Jeffersonian happiness. In the suburbs you weren't isolated as you were on the farm, and you weren't on top of one another as city dwellers were. You didn't have to produce your own food, because there were little shops (later malls) within easy driving distance, nor did you have to listen to the constant hum of commerce and industry right outside your front door. In this idyll, the yard was a personal preserve. The suburban yard was a slice of nature more personal than a city park, more convenient than the wilderness, and less demanding than a farm. There you could enjoy nature, even as you were grooming every inch of that nature to please your own tastes. Then you could sit back in a lawn chair with a cool drink and proudly survey your entire domain.

My father's relationship to his yard tended to be subtractive. Additive measures, such as planting flowers, held no interest for him. He appeared not to notice details like trees. His efforts were devoted to removing everything that got in the way of the immaculacy of the front lawn. He did the conventional chores, of course — mowing, raking leaves, moving the sprinkler around to even the greening. But he had a more uncommon preoccupation as well. He weeded crabgrass. He would position one wooden stake at the sidewalk, another at the rim of my mother's flower bed next to the house, and tie a string taut between them. Then he sat down in the grass and made his way methodically along this thin white disassembly line, working out weeds with his fingers and dropping them into a metal pail that he dragged along beside him. At the end of the row, he moved the stakes a few inches and started all over again. He never bothered with the backyard, since it was the front that others would see and judge him by.

He was not alone in his drive to put a good face on the front of the house. In every neighborhood we lived in, the front yard was a prime indicator of the inner well being of the family within. A lawn that was overgrown, even by an inch or two, provoked sarcastic comments from the fathers, who would meet informally at the curb over their lawn mowers and garden hoses. People who allowed their shrubbery to get shapeless or their children's toys to migrate to the front of the house were accused of bringing down the entire neighborhood. Even my grandmother Trebbe, who had almost nothing in common with my father and never spoke to him without a chill in her voice, saw things the same way. Whenever she came to visit, she made a point of bustling out the front door to rescue the flowerbeds from tiny weeds my mother had overlooked, chiding "Really, June, what will the neighbors think?"

There was an ethic not only for how the front yard was supposed to look, but also for how you ought to behave there. When adults were in the front yard they were performing public acts, of which there were but a tacitly approved few: washing the car, mowing the grass, trimming the shrubbery, welcoming and saying goodbye to guests. I remember passing through our kitchen once when my mother and a neighbor were drinking coffee in the "breakfast nook" and hearing them speak disapprovingly of a woman down the block who liked to sunbathe in a chaise longue on her front lawn. No one had to tell me what they meant. This woman, glistening with suntan oil in bathing suits the color of tropical fruits, lay baking for hours in the hot midwestern sun, showing too much flesh and not enough mobility. Her pastime would not have been worthy of mention if she had only taken her chaise around the corner to her own backyard. Sociologist William H. Whyte, who has studied people and their environments for decades, has observed that, while they are in the front yard, people are presumed to be accessible. Drawn to one another by their common activities, they will share tools, energy and advice in ways that gradually promote friendships. However, Whyte notes, "over-the-back-fence socializing" is the exception.

The backyard was the one that could be tailored to meet the needs of the individual family. Some next-door neighbors of ours in Omaha had turned their backyard into a work of landscape art, with a tiny pond complete with bridge, pathways bordered by flowers and miniature trees, and stones placed here and there with clear deliberation. In an earlier neighborhood, we knew a large family whose backyard was crammed so full of swings, sandboxes, apparatus for all ball games, wading pools, and wheeled vehicles ranging from kiddie cars to two-wheeled bikes, that any blade of grass that dared show its head would have been trampled instantly. Another family, who did a lot of entertaining, not only had a flagstone patio and a set of matching lawn furniture, they had even strung an electrical cord around the periphery of the backyard, and hung Japanese paper lanterns on it for parties, decor I envied mightily.

As for me, I went to my backyard to find wilderness. The grownups' zeal to suppress the sprouting of things seemed foolish to me. I loved my backyards because they showed me that nature was by nature rampant and bold and would always manage to poke through wherever it could, no matter how small the plot of earth or what efforts were undertaken to prune it back. A weed would find a crack in the driveway and burrow in. Dandelions and violets bloomed in the grass just days after my father had beheaded them with the lawn mower. Each element of the yard, moreover, was a discrete habitat with mysteries all its own, and any bird, bug or weather pattern that spent time there contributed its own feisty way of getting on with life. In the winter, when I crawled beneath the snow-slung branches of the Norway spruce beside our driveway, I stepped into a place as little explored as a ice floe in the Arctic. It was so confining there that I could hardly adjust my knees without bumping the boughs and bringing a cascade of snow down on myself, but all I had to do was move my head a fraction of an inch from side to side to witness rainbows flaring from ice crystals on the tips of the needles. In the summer, I glided among the fronds of our weeping willow tree, talking to myself as I invented stories in which jungle vines or magical, fluttering curtains were prominent features. I chased fireflies through familiar distances distorted by their teasing lights, watched ants fight long after they had torn each others' legs off, and saw two sparrows mate on the picnic table with a passion so grand they thrust themselves onto the grass.

I spent so much time in my landscapes of narrow boundaries that I came to see each element as an ally that was not only alive, but fully aware of my presence within it and glad to have me. This lush world trusted me enough to show me its mysteries and I paid close attention. I learned that every living thing in my backyard was madly making a home for itself.

Caring not a whit for propriety, everything fought or fled, struck down roots, turned invisible or played dead so as to hold its place and protect its young and its next burst of growth. It was as if each element, including rocks and rain puddles, grasped the imminence of its own demise and was fully prepared to resist that end. In the meantime, a creature lived beautifully, claiming space and growing wildly.

Once, I opened the door that led from the backyard into the garage and startled a bird that had gotten trapped there. My intrusion reminded it of its predicament and, all wings and urgency, it flapped into the darkness that smelled of motor oil and old tires and hurled itself against the pane of one of the two small windows leading out to the side yard. It thumped repeatedly at this false exit, then swooped around the garage a few more times, acquiring energy or resolve, before throwing itself at the window again. The spectacle enthralled and horrified me. There was no refinement in this bird, none of the easy social skills birds like to exhibit when they are in their own environment. I held the door open for it and stood aside, but it would not take a chance. This, too, I found remarkable. A bird who could zip unerringly into a nesting hole beneath the eaves or land without tottering on a twig would not go through a wide door when its life depended on it. It just kept pounding at that pane of sky as if one time it might find the glass had melted and it could sail right through. I realized that it was prepared to bash its brains out to get its freedom back, and I half hoped to see it happen. I was curious to know just how punishing such madness could get.

I watched until I scared myself, for I was beginning to fathom some territory I did not want to approach too closely. I slipped out and ran around to the driveway in front of the house, where I heaved the big garage door open. Immediately the bird saw the light and flew through. I knew as its wingbeats steadied and regained control that it was already forgetting what had befallen it, and for this I felt sorrow, envy, and contempt.

As much as I dabbled with the wild in my suburban environment, I was also acutely conscious of the people who lived around me. Indeed, if the neighbors had their eye on us, as my family suspected, I was watching back just as attentively.

I was five when we moved from Indianapolis to Springfield, Illinois. For a year or so, while I went to kindergarten, we lived in a house that had a huge catalpa tree with woody pods that made an exotic music in the wind. Then my father decided to build us a house of our own. He bought a lot in a housing development, the kind that was spreading all over America in the Fifties, as prairies, farms and animal habitats were plowed under to create "Meadowbrook Acres," "Whispering Hills" and "Robinwood." My father made our house from scratch. He took me to see it one day. There were no front steps, so we entered our front door by walking up a ramp of plywood boards to the stoop. My father led me from room to room, filling me in on what each would become: living room, kitchen, my room, my little brother Frederick's room. All of the house's innards were bared. Behind the bathroom walls, the pipes were round and smooth as guts. Wires, still unattached to their source of power, dangled out of holes in the ceilings. In places, the floor dropped clear through to the basement, from which wafted the smell of concrete, cool, damp and earthy. I felt privileged to know my future home so intimately, and was proud of my father for having created it for us.

When I saw it next it was finished, and it looked like every other house on the block, except for its color. Our house was white. Our neighbors to the left, the Rockfords, were the blue house; the Clarks, to the right, were beige. My best friend Ann Hubbard's house, directly across the street, was red. The Pages, who had a tank of tropical fish that my friend Danny and I fed to death one afternoon, lived in a gray house. There was a spindly little tree in every front yard. In the back was a huge field, one remnant of the farm the place had been. Wild asparagus grew there, and rabbits hopped wickets through the grass.

My mother was unhappy in that house. She complained because there were no trees, and because the landscape was so flat. She hated the anonymity of the homes. I kept to myself the things I loved about it. One day, for instance, I had a spiritual experience in my backyard, or rather, just beyond it, in the field. A few days before Halloween, I lay there on my back in the tall grass, determined to watch without blinking as the sky changed from afternoon azure to twilight blue. Although I didn't succeed, I would continue to look to the natural world for clues to linking up with the great mystery.

I was fascinated by the sameness of the houses on our street, for each was a mirror of my own. In Ann's house you turned left to get to the bedrooms, whereas in ours you turned right. When you stood at her kitchen sink, which looked exactly like our kitchen sink, you saw another block of houses; in ours you saw the field. And when you looked out the picture window in Ann's living room, you saw our picture window staring back. I had many friends in this neighborhood and spent time in many houses, and I felt I understood something of the inner workings of all of them. My new school was just a few blocks away. There is a snapshot of me with Danny and Ann, Terry of the blue house next to us, and Tommy of the yellow house a few doors down, walking down the middle of the street on our first day of first grade, five little Baby Boomers taking big solo steps into the wide world.

In the summer, we had block parties. The men put sawhorses at the intersections to cut off the light traffic that turned our way and set up their barbecue grills in a clump in the street. Every family contributed chairs and card tables, which they arranged in two long parallel rows. The fathers grilled hamburgers and hot dogs, and the mothers brought out bowls of potato salad, coleslaw and Jell-o molds filled with canned fruit cocktail and tiny marshmallows. Big garbage pails held beer and sodas packed in ice that melted as the party went on. The street became a concourse, a living room, a kitchen and playground all in one. On one of these occasions, after night had fallen and the littlest children had been put to bed in two or three adjacent houses, so their parents could tend them easily, I stood on my own front lawn and saw before me my entire neighborhood, collected. The young people were on one half of the street playing softball, the adults on the other, lingering at the tables, talking and laughing. Behind them all were the houses, mostly dark now, for we had all been outside for hours. The screen doors and windows of the houses were open, so the soft night within the rooms flowed out, and the good mood flowed in. I could pick out the voices of my parents, not too loud, not too sustained, not even my father's, which had a tendency to crash through every other voice when he'd had too much to drink. The hungry smells of beer and charcoal briquettes were muted at this short distance by the scent of cut grass, and the scents, like the voices, folded gently in upon one another, so nothing sharp was allowed to protrude.

I wanted to preserve this moment forever. More, I wanted to give it room to grow. I began to skip from one front yard to the next. I skipped to the far end of the street, crossed, and skipped back up the lawns on the other side, then back to my side again and down to the end of the street again. Round and round and round I went, spinning a huge oval as my feet touched grass and concrete, grass and concrete, and my arms swung wide. I skipped until I was breathless, and still kept going, as if my life depended on this ritual by which I might touch, on the one hand, all the sweet conviviality within the circle, and on the other, the open, welcoming homes without, so that I could hold both of them and make them accessible to all of us whenever we needed them.

My father was transferred to Omaha in the spring I was in second grade. He had high expectations for this move. He would be in charge of several branch offices and would have more people working, as he put it, "under him." Usually, when he came home from work, he would sit in the kitchen with my mother while she cooked dinner, sipping a cocktail and complaining about the men he worked with. Now he was full of optimism. He looked forward to starting anew. This meant more than setting a fresh set of goals and striding forth to attain them; it also meant burying the past, as if what had gone before was just a flawed prelude, best forgotten, to what he was going to accomplish now that all the right elements were in place.

So Omaha was going to make all the difference. He promised we would have a big house there, with a big yard, and that we might even be able to get a horse. While my parents were looking for the new place, we moved for a spring and summer into a cramped, dark rental house, where I had to share a bedroom with my little brother. The backyard was a tiny grassless scrap with one tree in the center of it. One side of the yard was bordered by a ditch of overgrown weeds, the other by a chainlink fence behind which paced a suspicious German shepherd. I missed our street in Springfield. There was no place to be alone.

I solved the problem by moving into the tree. Every afternoon when I got home from school, I would pack a book, a stuffed animal, a piece of toast and other necessities into an old fake-leopardskin purse of my mother's and hoist myself up onto a sturdy branch. Before long, I was rewarded for my faith, for the tree turned out to be a cherry and began flowering all around me. The old tale of the guest who is received with kindness by simple people in their cottage and who then reveals his true identity as a god was reversed: now it was the humble home that turned out to be divine and the guest who had the apotheosis. In this lacy kingdom I flourished. I decorated myself with blossoms of such fine shading that I had to study them to decipher where the white left off and the pink began. I peeled back curls of stippled bark and smelled and tasted it and made miniature villages out of it. I observed how the blossoms bloomed and wilted, pried globules of amber sap off the trunk, rolled them soft in my fingers and used them to stick the pictures I drew onto the branches. I read, I ate my toast. I looked down upon my house and the neighbors and the pacing dog and smiled pityingly, as the angels would, upon their ignorance.

When summer came and school ended, the blossoms dropped and the tree put all its energy into the making of fruit. The cherries were disappointingly tasteless, but I was proud of my tree for its feat and ate them anyway. Frederick and I played peasant-in-the-vineyard, stomping cherries with our bare feet and singing loudly. We had cherry fights, made ourselves up like clowns with red cherry cheeks, got cherries all over ourselves, our clothes and the kitchen floor. Finally, my mother told my father he had to "do something" about the cherries. He made a Saturday morning project of it. He scooped shovels full of cherries from under the tree, loaded them into the wheelbarrow, rolled the wheelbarrow over to the ditch and tipped it. Finally, he covered the ditch with grass clippings. I watched the whole thing from my bedroom window. I grieved for the tree, shunned as soon as its fairy tale beauty turned sticky and it lacked the strength to hold tight to the fruits of its unrestrained profligacy. The final insult was the relegation of the cherries to the ditch, as if by simply covering up the mess my parents could stanch the flow for good. I took vengeful delight in the sight of a couple of cherries plopping down on the lawn even before my father had put his tools away.

We did not get the horse or the pasture-sized backyard I'd pictured us and the horse living on. Instead, we moved to a white upper-middle class Omaha neighborhood, where two-story homes were surrounded by big lawns with big old trees, and boundaries were marked by tall privet hedges, a subtler device for keeping the neighbors at a distance than a chainlink fence. Our house, made of honey-colored bricks, was on a corner, with a front and back yard and a huge side yard. My mother loved the house. She planted flowers in the yard, and she made friends among the women who lived nearby. My father, however, changed for the worse.

The seventh of eight children, he had not wanted to stay in Texas and work the poor, dusty soil, as four generations of his family had done before him. He dreamed of being a lawyer. At the age of nineteen, he entered the University of Texas, and thought he was on his way. But after two years, lack of money or lack of faith in himself forced him to drop out. He got a job with Aetna Insurance and stuck with it for the next forty years, a career man to the core in the days when that kind of loyalty could be counted on to pay off. But, although he hid it under a booming Texas-style bravado, his background and his missed opportunities haunted him. He worried that people did not respect him as they ought to; he worried that he was not worthy of respect. And he was married to a woman whose very presence reminded him of what he was not. The daughter of an actor and an artist's model, my mother had gained certain skills of gentility, such as impeccable taste in furniture and clothes, summers spent at the Connecticut shore, and an easy grace with big cities and famous people. My parents met at the Arthur Murray School of Dance, where she was a teacher and he her pupil. They were not happy. They had little in common except a fondness for working, never together, in the yard, and a tacit compact to blind themselves to the truth about what was happening to our family.

Although my father longed for the trappings of success, he was not sure how to use them, and he resented those who could. When he chatted with the men who were our new neighbors — the architect next door, the doctor down the street, the corporate executive whose backyard pool I learned to swim in — he was jovial and outgoing. In fact, he could interrupt a tirade against my mother, my brother, or me and metamorphose with fearful skill into a genial family man if someone we knew happened to drive by. But at night, when he was drinking, he criticized these people, accused them of putting on airs, of thinking themselves better than he.

In this neighborhood, I was not as outgoing as I had been in Springfield. I stopped inviting school friends over the day I tried to hustle a friend past my father, home unexpectedly from a business trip and sitting in the living room drinking gin martinis. He refused to let us go upstairs until I had said hello to him in just the cheerful and respectful tone he demanded, an exercise I had to repeat several times before he was satisfied. After that I went to other people's houses, or stayed in my own backyard, where I could keep an eye on my mother. But it was a splendid yard with many terrains that I made my own: a sprawling lilac bush; the willow, with its long fronds; the privet hedge, so dense I could lie on top of it; a birdbath and a small curved bench carved out of stone; even a little white tool shed with two windows and a glass doorknob that I begged my father to turn into a playhouse for me. Even when my mother and father were out in the yard, I felt comfortably private as I wandered among these microcosmic habitats, talking to myself, inventing, moving in.

My father was often away on business trips. When he was home he drank, and his drinking became more and more violent. I trained myself to be a light sleeper, so I could hear the silences downstairs as plain as the shouts and the shattering china, for he tried to attack my mother quietly, so as not to wake us children up, and she complied by defending herself in whimpers. But I could sense trouble through my skin and would run downstairs to find him punching her or pounding her head against the two walls of a far corner of the living room. I pleaded with him or, when that didn't work, beat him on the back with my fists. If he still wouldn't stop, I phoned the police. We could tell they had arrived when the flashing red light from their car splashed against the living room curtains, and by the time they knocked on the front door, my father had composed himself. He adopted a slurred, man-to-man affability: there was nothing to worry about, a little disagreement between him and his wife, that was all. His daughter, who had bothered the officers, was just high-strung and ought to be in bed. Often, my mother conspired, assuring them she was fine. Some of those policemen believed them; others, I could tell, did not and would genuinely have liked to help us. But this was in the late Fifties, when fathers were presumed to know best and the law declined to intervene in "domestic quarrels."

After they left, my father's outrage mushroomed, for now he had been publicly humiliated on top of all his other woes. The attack against my mother resumed. It was at this point that she would tell me to go upstairs and wake Frederick. It never failed to break my heart to do so. He looked so innocent lying on his stomach and cuddling his terrycloth dog. Holding his hand, I took him downstairs. Then he and our mother and I would race out of the house and across the yard, all its intimate features gone black and dangerous as we skirted obstacles and slipped on the wet grass, fleeing my father, who stood in the lighted doorway and screamed into the night, "June! Get back here!"

Often we ran across the side yard, ducking through the gap in the corner of the privet hedge that Frederick and I used as a shortcut to our friends' houses. Sometimes we went only as far as the Wertzes', the home next door with the landscaped garden. Ginny Wertz was pretty and slim and had no children, a status I found both perplexing and glamorous. When we stayed there, I slept on a floral couch on the sunporch, where I was surrounded by windows that looked out onto the sleeping garden. I could lie there and watch the progress of the moon from one side of the windows to the other. Other times we knocked on the Witherspoons' door. They lived a couple of houses down from the Wertzes and had two little boys. Mrs. Witherspoon's first name was Hlois, pronounced with a breathy first letter, and she had a halo of bright red hair like Little Orphan Annie's. She led us up to a guest room decorated in a shade of blue the color of icicles on a winter afternoon. The bedspreads were satiny and there was a blue velvet armchair where I would have liked to spend hours reading. Some nights we ran over the front lawn, which my father had groomed so carefully that the neighbors might think well of us, and across the street to the Bernards' house. Lorraine Bernard, a tall, dark-haired woman with a bold laugh and a long stride, touched her finger to her lips as we tiptoed down the carpeted hall to my friend Linda's room. Quietly, so as not to wake Linda, I climbed into the twin bed and she tucked me in.

If these women shook their heads in bewilderment when they crawled back into bed beside their husbands, they never showed us anything but generosity. They opened their doors, they took clean sheets out of linen closets, they asked no questions. They were the best of neighbors. I was ashamed of our repeated need to make these visits, and said little while we were getting settled. Once I lay in my temporary bed, however, I kept myself awake, not out of fear this time, but in order to luxuriate in the commodious safety. I knew there was no danger that my father would bother us; he wouldn't have wanted anyone to think he was the kind of man who had to go out searching for his wife. I lay memorizing the details of these serene rooms, pretending they were mine and trying to breathe like a person who possessed such a space. I always hoped that my mother would get the message too, that it would dawn on her that people could live quiet, lovely lives and that she could leave my father and make a new home for us. But although she glimpsed the possibilities often enough, she was like that bird in the garage; she kept on slamming herself right back into the only vista that looked familiar.

We left at dawn, so we could get back home before anyone spied us out in public in our pajamas. As we nervously neared the house, I looked around at my yard and felt old, wise, and battered, as if I knew far more of life than the trees and birds and sunshine nonchalantly conducting their morning business. Sometimes we found my father passed out in the living room or even on the front seat of the car, as if he had been in a hurry to make a getaway. Often, he was sitting morosely at the dining room table, drinking coffee and watching out the window for our return. He gathered us to him, put his arms around us, and told us how sorry he was. He promised he would never drink again and we pretended to believe him.

After I grew up and had a yard of my own to care for, I began to wonder if my father's ministrations to the lawn may have had a purpose beyond convincing the neighbors that he was just as fine a citizen as they. Maybe he got some satisfaction from the practice itself. Weeding was one facet of his life over which he had perfect control: he could isolate a section of the lawn and, using his length of string as a gauge, create a manageable course of action for himself. Then, with care and discipline, he could locate every single defect that marred the pristine whole and yank it out by the roots. Every detail that failed to fit into his vision of how things ought to be was eradicated. The weeds would return, but they were his weeds, he knew them intimately and he knew exactly how to deal with them. And anyway, he liked starting over, believing with every fresh effort that this would be the time when everything, finally, turned out right. Perhaps he dreamed of a day when he could store his string and stakes and pail in the garage for good, and the lawn, his purest and most praiseworthy endeavor, would thrive on its own.

As a child, I was embarrassed by my father's weeding. The way I saw it, the lawn was a vast place that demanded expansive gestures; weeding crabgrass by hand seemed an act of disproportionate puniness. Besides, nobody else's father sat hunched for hours over his front yard. One day, however, shortly before my parents finally separated, I rounded the hedge after school, saw him at his task and, inexplicably, felt love for him. Maybe a success at school or some expression of sixth-grade friendship had suffused me with a warmth that still radiated. Or maybe the fact that I was approaching him from the outside world, a day traveler about to enter his domain voluntarily, made me believe for a moment that I also had the option of walking away. He wore an old tan work shirt and khaki pants, and he sat in the grass with one leg crossed before him, the other bent near his chin so he could rest an elbow on his knee. The fingers of his right hand pursed the grass. He looked enrapt, this man who so needed to be important now bent humbly over the soil. And it came to me that maybe he loved the yard the same way I did.

I decided to find out, a proposition I knew was risky. First, of course, I was afraid of him. Second, he had no idea how to talk to us children. He could not conceive that we had psyches of our own and accused us of getting our opinions, and even our memories of the things he did when he was drunk, from someone else. Third, I did not want to give away any secrets. To reveal my true relationship to the yard would have been tantamount to giving him access to it, a privilege he was capable of dishonoring, as he had proved when he violated the cherry tree. I can't remember what I said. Maybe I complimented him on how much crabgrass filled the pail, or told him I was glad he was home early. Maybe my opening gambit was a comment about how nice it felt to sit in the grass. What I said, I probably said with dense ambiguousness. There was a silence. Then my father made some jovial remark that gave no clue that he had heard even the superficial version of my invitation. If he harbored a secret friendship with his earth, he was not about to confess it to me. I was abashed. But I had learned from his example how to cover my insecurities; I mentioned casually that I had homework to do and sauntered off. Still, I like to think he not only heard, but knew what I meant and yearned to respond. After all, up until the time he died, when I was in my thirties, he kept evoking that first occasion, which I was too young to remember, when I had reached out him over the yard and he had been filled with delight.

THE COAL REMEMBERS

This creek has some kind of gumption. That's my reaction as I consider Sterry Creek, rippling along through the woodland between banks of refuse and neglect. Near its eastern bank a bare, black hill of coal waste hunches its shoulders against the blue October sky. To the west, the woods along the pitted and stony track I'm walking are scattered with more contemporary trash: a weather-ravaged mattress; cans and brushes left over from a paint job, laid out with anomalous tidiness on a blue plastic tarp; shiny clots of fused stuff; lumber; tires and more tires. And yet, on flows the creek, as if it has somewhere to get to and is so intent on its journey that it bothers little about the detritus it must pass along the way. Narrow and clear, it lifts and shuffles cast-offs as if they were no more noxious than autumn leaves. As the sports writer, Broadway personality, and author of *Guys & Dolls*, Damon Runyon, once quipped about the grass that managed to grow among the cracks of sidewalks in New York City, this creek has "moxie."

The big heap gleaming like an obsidian mountain range in the late afternoon sun is called a "culm bank." It's composed of shale, sandstone, and other unsalable tailings that were removed from the ore during the coal boom in the 1920s, 30s, 40s, and 50s, and it's one of hundreds left throughout anthracite coal country here in northeastern Pennsylvania. Although local families regard the culm banks as testaments to the hard work that their parents and grandparents from Wales, Poland, Italy, Ireland, and other countries came here to live and die in service of, the implications of them, if not the mounds themselves, are monstrous when you actually pause before them to gaze and consider. Which, for those of us who live in this region, is easy to avoid doing, since they are almost as much a part of the landscape as their daintier cousins, the green hills known as the Endless Mountains that start rolling north just a few miles from here. You get so used to coal waste that it ceases to be shocking, as some new ecological outrage would be, something like a city block blown-out by a bomb, or the charred skeletons of houses and trees ravaged by wildfire, or like the hole that opened up in 1903 in the town of Olyphant, at whose southern end this coal patch lies. When a ceiling of the mine collapsed, it swallowed the West End Hotel, pulled the walls of several neighboring buildings below ground, and snapped the water main.

Over the decades, thirty thousand people died working in Pennsylvania's anthracite mines, and yet the mining went on, and the culm banks peaked higher and higher. How many men, boys, mules, and vehicles, I wonder, must have labored up those slopes on the other side of the creek to erect such a store of blatant undesirability. The women of the mining families would have picked over it in search of overlooked lumps of coal that they could carry back to heat their small and insubstantial company homes. The mound is a wound on the current landscape and a scar of the past. And yet the features that frame it include, right before me, a scrim of thistles, goldenrod, milkweed, and tall grasses, all in their mid-autumn fuzziness, and on the far side of the coal, the gold, crimson, and copper chenille of trees at their picturesque peak. Like the creek, they prevent me from assuming a stance of unmitigated sorrow or indignation about this place. It's not pretty. And then again, it kind of is.

Behind me the traffic on Route 6 murmurs and coughs, while crickets offer a friendly, pre-frost greeting in the scrub. Along both sides of the track, trees of a variety surprising for a waste place shimmer in the breeze, and leaves sashay through the air onto the ground: golden tulip trees and mitten-shaped sassafras, red maple, ochre birch, leathery oak and ash. Flycatchers flit among the sunny leaves of poplars, commenting briefly to one another. Purple wild asters, yellow partridge pea with its showy red stalk, and the miniature daisies of fleabane are still blooming in patches of sunlight. Abruptly the soil under my boots shifts from powdery and dough-colored to gritty black. I've seen photos of the Earth below the surface here, so I can picture the way the pale sandstone is laced with dark veins of coal, one of which I've obviously just stepped upon. Olyphant is near the tip of Pennsylvania's northernmost anthracite coalfield, which curves out from Carbondale in a long, thin shape, roughly resembling a pea pod, to taper off again at the town of Shickshinny about fifty miles southwest. Three other patches of anthracite, looking like the smears of a Rorschach test, lie just to the south of where this one ends. I'm not walking on solid ground. Beneath my feet gape the spaces made by the removal of the billions of tons of stuff that have wafted into America's skies in coal-heated stoves and furnaces. Underground stretch labyrinthine passageways constructed in a pattern called "room-and-pillar." The "rooms" were spaces cut into the rock, while the "pillars" were those parts of the substratum left untouched, so as to keep the whole architecture from collapsing. The miners worked these tunnels ten hours a day six days a week. When a man died, his body would be dumped in front of the small house he rented from the coal company. Everyone in the family knew that if they didn't find a replacement for him within a few days, they'd be kicked out of their home. Little boys as young as seven worked as "breakers" for pennies a week, bent over those rocks that never ceased to pile up before them, as they sorted the lumps into different sizes and picked out the waste that would add to the culm.

When the steep path reaches the far end of the culm bank on the other side of the creek, and the terrain to my left opens up into woods, a sense of relief floods me, as if both the land and I have been released from a heavy burden. A large puddle lies to the side of the path, and an animal trail bypasses it and curls into the woods. Glossy black against its base of coal and tessellated with scarlet, gold, and bronze leaves, the surface of the puddle looks like fine Japanese laquerware. A large emerald dragonfly darts purposefully among several invisible mid-air ports of call. One of the rewards of spending time with waste places is the startlement of beauty they hold in reserve. They take what has happened to them and deal with it. They are pushy and creative, and they muddle through, working with what they've got without expecting any favors. There is much to discover, both in the land and in myself, whenever I step into the mystery of a place that's been through a lot of trials, yet I almost always postpone the journey. The neurons in my brain that respond to my anticipation of visiting a new place sparkle a lot more brightly if I'm considering an old-growth forest or a winding trail in the Utah Canyonlands than when I'm heading off to explore a gas fracking site, a municipal dump, or this bleak reminder of Pennsylvania's past as "King of Coal." On some level, I know that if I allow myself to truly experience what is before me, my worldview will be rattled in ways I can't anticipate. I will, at the very least, be forced to experience something, perhaps uncomfortable, in the tender inner frontier where "I" meet "other." Today my mission is just to absorb what is. I must greet and engage with this place in its integrity, as I do whenever I settle in to a shy first encounter with what the philosopher Emmanuel Levinas called "the vulnerable face of the other."

Behind me climbs a grinding roar, unmistakably the sound of an all-terrain vehicle. As it approaches, I step off the path into the trees to wait out its passage. The ATV shoots up the track below, then jerks to a halt as the incline steepens. The driver, a man whose age is indeterminate behind his helmet, backs the vehicle up slightly, then detonates it forward again. I press my hands against my ears as it screams up the slope. The driver glances my way, offers a quick wave, which I return, and tears up the hill without losing any more momentum.

The sun is getting low in the sky, but I keep walking, determined at least to give a nod to the other culm bank I've come to see before turning back. And just moments later I arrive, not at my destination, but at a clear sign of its proximity. The track diverges a short way off to the right and comes to a sudden end before a tall chain-link fence. Behind it the added prohibition of a camera mounted on a tall pole warns me that trying to proceed will not be tolerated. I smell smoke. Or I think I smell smoke. Lifting my head like a deer, I sniff and sniff again, but it could be that the scent I'm gleaning is only decaying leaves or maybe just imagination. Then again, it really could be smoke, because although the vista behind the fence is an innocuous stand of young poplars shimmying in the breeze, I know that this fence marks the boundaries of an underground coal fire. I'm tempted to follow the fence a little farther, but the sun is already glowing through the trees in the western woods, so I return to the main track and turn around. Before getting back in the car, I turn and make a deep bow to the whole place.

And after my first visit, I find I am intrigued. I can't wait to go back to the coal patch. First, however, I want to learn more of the background of the place.

The only furniture in this narrow, windowless room of the Bureau of Abandoned Mine Reclamation in Wilkes-Barre is a very long span of tables running down the middle, with chairs on either side. Clearly this is no ideal arrangement for a conference or a brainstorming session among colleagues; it's meant for independent study. Affixed to the wall behind the chairs are waist-high racks from which hang large folios depicting the interiors of the region's coal mines. Mining Engineer Dan Werner has selected one, Folio 10X, and laid it out on the table, but before he opens it, we bend over a smaller portrait of Olyphant's mines, an aerial photograph. Several patches of the land below the highway, dark woodland green interrupted by two gray humps of culm piles, are marked with yellow outlines. Each one, Dan explains, is known as a "PA," a Problem Area. The problems include subsidence, dangerous high walls, leftover refuse, clogged stream channels, old slopes, and the biggest problem of all, the underground mine fire.

It started in 2004, when somebody decided that a culm bank would be a great place for setting an old car on fire. The fire did what it could with steel and rubber, then moved on to embrace a more compatible partner. Down into the coal mine it slipped and outwards toward the town of Dunmore to the west. Coal burns slowly, at the rate of about one foot per day, but even when it's slow, contained, and invisible, a culm fire is toxic, for it emits greenhouse gases, as well as carbon monoxide, hydrogen sulfide, and various trace elements. In an effort to contain the damage, the Office of Surface Mining dug a U-shaped trench 150 feet deep and 2,800 feet long and lined it with clay. That prevented the fire from spreading horizontally, but it's still smoldering throughout an estimated seven acres at temperatures ranging from fifty degrees Fahrenheit to more than four hundred degrees.

Northeastern Pennsylvania's mining industry ceased almost completely after 1959, when miners, under orders, dug too close to the banks of the Susquehanna River. The river breached the mine and the tunnels flooded, killing twelve people and injuring dozens more. Decades later, many mines farther south are still under water. Higher elevations in the north have kept Olyphant's mine dry but more susceptible to fire. The coal veins are also thinner here, as I see when Dan peels back the cover of Folio 10X. On each large page is a floor plan of one level of a particular section of the mine, each room and pillar meticulously drawn. Olyphant's folio contains only three pages. The folios of mines father south, Dan explains, comprise eight or nine pages, each one representing a level deeper than the one above it. Around the town of Shamokin, the miners would have descended more than five hundred feet into the Earth each day to do their jobs. The neat diagrams on the page reveal nothing of mining's daily narrative of dirt, danger, and strain. The miners and their families lived with aching muscles, fatigue, debt to the company store, and the awareness that their children would likely grow up to the same existence. Because the miners spoke so many different languages, messages, including urgent ones, sometimes couldn't be communicated. But then again, I have to assume that a camaraderie beyond words bonded these men, children, and women who lived their lives with coal.

These days, the only thing that's moving through those rooms and breaking them up is fire. The plan, Dan says, is to dig out the uncombusted coal and extinguish the fire, then fill in the trenches and reclaim the land and about seventy-five acres surrounding it, so it can be converted, perhaps to an industrial park. When that work might begin is unknown. Meanwhile, although mining in this region ended decades ago, the coal itself does not stand idle. Abandoned, it is yet active. Like Sterry Creek, like poplar trees sprouting in a black bed of carbon, and a dragonfly busy with the air over a puddle, the coal in the mine goes ahead and goes on, doing what it does well. It burns.

A few days after my visit to the Bureau of Abandoned Mine Reclamation, I return to the coal patch. This time I take a different path, less traveled and surrounded by woods. It, too, is littered with trash. Off to the side of the rutted path, an old wooden door has been propped up against a fallen tree. Someone has nailed a paper plate to the door and used it for target practice. Although riddled with bullet holes, the plate is still white and untouched by weather, implying that the presence of this other visitor is as fresh as the fallen leaves I've crunched through. Farther, other dumpers have gone to more trouble to make their trash vanish. They've maneuvered their vehicles along this narrow, bumpy track several hundred feet from the road and then pitched their refuse down the side of the hill. A child's pink plastic pedal car lies among a dozen plastic grocery story bags, their handles knotted up to keep the contents inside. As I watch, leaves drift down from the trees to slip and slide over the sides of the bags and pad the molded pink interior of the little car. For a moment I despise these waste bearers who go to such trouble to inflict their undesirables on this place that is doing its best to recover. Indignant, I picture myself riffling through the trash until I come up with a culpable envelope that exposes their identity and then doing something righteous and punitive, like phoning them and letting them know they've been fingered or tossing the garbage back on their lawn.

Waste attracts more waste. When a place is seen as useless, unwanted, uncared for, it loses value not just once but increasingly over time. It becomes a pariah of the landscape. Almost, it becomes execrable. Before long it is no longer a place in need of attention but a repository for other things that have passed from usefulness to junk. Once so condemned, it invites deliberate acts of aggression and disrespect, such as target practice, dumping trash, and setting an old car on fire. The place has become good for nothing—nothing except expressions of contempt. And, I have to admit as I settle down from my reaction to the trash, it can also provoke spite on the part of those of us who think ourselves more virtuous stewards of the land.

Higher, the path ends at another section of that forbidding chain-link fence. Although no camera peers down at me here, concertina wire blocks any attempt to gain access. Animals have made a track around the foot or so of roughly horizontal land around the fence, as if they were pilgrims circumambulating a sacred mountain. Although the woods to my right are thick and the slope steep, I can amble along in a counterclockwise direction with no problem at all until I come to a large maple tree that has crashed down and completely blocked passage. Its upper branches have bent the top of the fence, and briefly my imagination plays with the possibility of climbing diagonally up through the branches and into the fire area. Instead I bushwhack downhill through to where the roots of the overturned tree form a wall of mud and stone parallel to the metal fence. A scattering of boulders nearby makes a good place to sit, so I do. Again I'm reminded of Levinas and his writing about the open, needy face of the *other*. When I let myself be drawn into the vulnerability that's communicated beneath first impressions of the one before me, I soften. My defenses slip. It dawns on me that, wherever I look, I will see a life that is etched with some hurt, even if the scars aren't always visible. It's true of places no less than people. In that suffering and survival, I see beauty and discover something like love. No doubt about it, I now love this coal patch. Before I leave, I weave dried flowers, leaves, and a blue jay feather into the fence as a parting gift.

My reflection on that second visit that the trail around the fence was like a path of circumambulation around a sacred place gives me an idea I can't shake. "Circumambulate the fence!" I scrawl on a Post-it and stick on my computer. By the time my schedule permits such a pilgrimage, it's early November, and the sky over Olyphant is temperamental, reeling from overcast to bright sun and occasionally releasing flurries of snow. The puddles I sidled around on my previous walks are covered with a thin layer of ice. Except for the oak and a few enthusiastically twirling poplars, the trees are bare. Under the windy gray sky the culm bank broods ominously.

I will say this about that walk: there is surprising beauty and gargantuan scarring. The land is busy the entire time. And my mood gets whipped around as wildly by the terrain as the trees are jostled by the wind. Just seconds after I begin my walk, clockwise this time, around the fence and I'm pushing through a thicket of spindly cherry trees, I spot a large silver Christmas tree ornament glistening in a sudden shower of sun. It's the size of a grapefruit and perfectly intact except for two small holes in its thin crust. How did a Christmas ornament come to be here? By wind? Dumped? How is it possible that it is so little battered after all it must have been through to get from somebody's holiday tree to the coal patch? Picking it up and nestling it in my backpack, I feel gleeful and triumphant, as if my good intentions for making this odd solo pilgrimage have been noted and applauded. Pride shifts into aesthetic appreciation as the hill levels off into a flat area, where poplars with white trunks and buttercup yellow leaves sprout from the ebony coal floor sparkling on both sides of the fence. Deducing at first that coal is no deterrent to growth, I begin to grasp that all these trees are young, a clue that their ambition does not match their ability to mature in such soil. Another culm bank broods nearby and I can see several more behind it.

As I peer at the vista through the fence, four ravens glide overhead, playing with the wind and one another. One veers over to investigate me. The birds drift onward when I make the turn to walk the far southern side of the fence, and at that moment the sun disappears behind a cloud. Thickets of blackberries now knot my path. Instantly I feel abandoned and edgy. I start worrying about people with guns and ATVs and other hobbies of messy destruction. I chastise myself for forgetting my orange vest when it's now two weeks into hunting season. As I press on, ducking through the thorns with eyes closed and head down, my nervous musings attach to a friend who's just been diagnosed with ovarian cancer.

On the long western side of the fence the landscape inside the containment changes abruptly. Just a few feet away from me tower mounds of coal waste thirty or forty feet high. Deep pits run among them. There is no scent of burning, no sign of smoke, but knowing that this is the place where fire is slowly devouring the substrata is like standing at the site of a recent highway accident or act of violence: the terrible reality of the unseen coats the place, blotting out the apparent ordinariness of what's before the eyes. Something grave and relentless is happening here. The fire in this colliery is one of an estimated forty burning in Pennsylvania's abandoned coal mines, both here in the east in anthracite country and in the western bituminous mines around Pittsburgh. Like the fuel rods of nuclear power plants, like garbage moldering in a landfill or sinking into a pile of autumn leaves, like carbon drifting into the skies and sticking there, the life of a thing does not easily vanish from the Earth just because humans are done with it. It lingers, it seeps, it clogs. What does one do with such a legacy? As I stand here looking in, my gloved fingers hooked round the metal mesh of the fence, snow flurries begin spinning through the air. This area of the coal patch is on the opposite side of the dirt track and remote from any other paths that can be trafficked. It is free, therefore, of trash except for the occasional windblown thing, like a cigarette pack or a damp gas station receipt. The overwhelming trace of human activity is the coal, the coal and the land's memory of the men and boys who disappeared into it each day to muscle their way through it and cart it up to the light.

The lines of a Yeats poem that have guided me for decades swim into my thoughts: "Now that my ladder's gone / I must lie down where all the ladders start / In the foul rag and bone shop of the heart." In other words, down at the bottom of as-bad-as-it-gets crouches the possibility of renewal. Compelled suddenly to make that paradox manifest, I take Yeats literally and lie down on the ground beside the fence. I'm half-hoping for another Christmas ornament moment — for the fire to reveal itself and radiate some gentle warmth over my back and legs, or at least for another flyover from ravens. It doesn't happen, of course. It never happens when you demand it. The ground is cold, the snow is brushing across my face, and the stones under the leaves make a punishing bed. Nevertheless, the very act of positioning myself here, supine on a place that's endured and still endures so many trials, shifts my relationship with it yet again. To lie down voluntarily on a place is to anticipate relief and solace. It's to take yourself off those resolute feet that hold you up and propel you all day long and give yourself over to a more extensive gravity.

I succumb to rest. Beneath me stretch loose stone, cold grasses, and a patchwork of rooms and pillars where many, many people did hard labor. If any of them ever lay down on the coal, they probably didn't do so by choice.

Farther along the fence, as I complete my circuit, there are more surprises: a shallow cave in a ledge of rock; a stretch of heath barrens at a high place on the path, where lichen embroiders a floor of chalk-white rock; a small pond, its cold mud impressed by the prints of deer, raccoon, turkey, and fox. The fence itself becomes an ally, as I grip the mesh to keep from slipping down the last steep and stony incline before arriving back at the gate.

The coal waste that lies scattered on the path and piled in the culm banks in this place is the Earth turned inside out, like the pocket of a jacket. Such places cause discomfort. They unabashedly expose, for any who cares to look, all that is foul, ugly, and spent, and maybe contagious as well. They don't keep their unpretty bits hidden, as one is taught to do in polite company. Yet waste places like this are teachers. Their wounds, and the deepening cuts that people continue to inflict upon them, reveal my own messy thoughts, such as paranoia, gloom, and a sudden hunger for vengeance. But they also coach me in how to persevere, no matter how bad it gets. They remind me that, if I'm a little bit patient, I'll quite possibly be granted a gift I can't possibly have earned. It could be a Christmas ornament, a dragonfly, or a moment of cold discomfort as I lie on the stony ground and picture the presence of those who toiled below. Most important, a waste place reveals that the memory of the Earth does not discriminate between beauty and ugliness, value and trash. This abandoned landscape remembers how to seed, flow, bloom, and chirp. The tunnels remember the many lives that labored and even laughed in them. The coal remembers how to smolder.

PART II

Teachers

ON THE MOORS OF OMAHA

I stepped outside and shut the door behind me, and the moors swept me into their updraft.

Space opens before her, resolute and uncontested under the sky The wind slaps at her cheeks, whips the long cape against her legs All around the grasses bend and recover with the gusts

Just across Western Avenue at 60th Street, the neighborhood made a quick transition from small ranch-style houses on small lots to larger ranch-style houses boasting lawns more spacious than garages and shaded by large trees.

If she were to turn around now, the ramshackle old house would look minuscule She will not turn At last she is alone with the land and sky Without slowing her pace, she heads up the nearest hill It is not the summit she craves, though, it's this movement of attaining it She is cold, out of breath, but she is not tired Instead, she finds the harassment of the wind, the demand of the slope exhilarating The moors join forces with her body and push her to keep going, for the more energy she puts into matching nature's rhythm, the more she forgets the restlessness burning in her heart

There were several options for turning right off 60th Street, and all of them led through Dundee, the stately neighborhood where the houses were brick with two or even three stories, big lawns, gardens, walls that made you wish to peek behind them, and windows into rooms where, now and then, you could gauge a personality from a glimpse of chair, a vase, a toy.

No matter how far she walks or how many summits she crests, the moors beckon her, even as they back away She knows the land is teasing her, knows that it wants her just as much as she wants it. It wants to be chased, and she's more than willing to give it that She strides toward the peak of the next hill

That was me at fifteen, walking the flat, tree-lined sidewalks of Omaha on my way to school. Since we had moved two years earlier to the duplex, where I lived with my mother, my grandparents, and my younger brother, I had loved my walk to and from school, for it offered a cradle of time and space where I could be alone without being an outcast and where I could indulge in imagining myself as someone other than who I was. I had several favorite houses on the route to school, and up until September of my sophomore year, I had amused myself by making up stories about the families who lived in them, and pretending that life was mine. But in recent weeks, my mind, if not my feet, had been covering new ground. Now, what I walked was the Yorkshire moors and with them some inkling of transcendence I could scarcely have put into words but was just beginning to glean. By the time I got to my school twenty minutes after leaving home, I was dazed, vague, elsewhere. The locker room, the bustle, the gossip of girls popped the spell. But, once again, I had found something on that walk, and it was all because of *Wuthering Heights*.

We had a new English teacher that year, a young woman named Miss Hansen, Lonnie Hansen. She was in her early twenties, a graduate of the University of Omaha, who had returned after spending a year in Europe. On the first day of school, she told us what to expect in her class during the coming year. We would be reading some of the great classics of world literature. Twice a year, we would each be assigned a book on which we would write a term paper. And every week, we would also be required to write an essay — she called it a "theme" — to be turned in on Friday. It felt scary and alluring. I couldn't wait.

All my life, I had been a reader. My mother used to say that when I was a baby, I would wake up early and start to cry, and she could get a little extra sleep and keep me happy if she just put a few picture books in my crib. She read to me when I was small, and by the time I was in kindergarten, I couldn't wait to learn how to read myself. The pace of the lessons in first grade frustrated me. On the first day of second grade, I had read the entire volume of our new Dick-Jane-and-Sally book by the time the bell rang.

It wasn't long before I realized that stories did not exist independently; they had makers: Laura Ingalls Wilder, C.S. Lewis, Rumer

Godden, Frances Hodgson Burnett, Beverly Cleary, Noel Streatfield, Elizabeth Headley, Rosamund du Jardin, and Janet Lambert. The presence of the author accompanied me throughout the reading of every book I checked out of the library. Just as the scenes of a book materialized in my imagination, sketchily detailed in the center, fuzzy at the edges, so an even fuzzier, but larger image of the author hovered over all the pages, looking critically down at them as if, even now, she were conjuring them, sentence by paragraph, into being. I began writing myself when I was about eight. Using the Aetna Insurance note pads my father brought home from the office, I wrote and illustrated little books about happy families and the things they did to move closer to some culminating happy event like Christmas day or a summer vacation in Sweden or Death Valley, places I studied wistfully in *The World Book Encyclopedia* and fantasized fleeing to, far from Omaha. Now that I was in high school, I often pretended, while doing my homework, that I was an adult living in New York and working on a feature story for *Newsweek*.

The first novel Miss Hansen assigned was *Wuthering Heights* by Emily Brontë, published in 1847 when its author was twenty-nine. I still have that Airmont Books paperback. In the middle of an ochre-colored border an oval contains what is meant to be a portrait of Cathy and Heathcliff. Behind Heathcliff, the sky is dark and stormy, while the backdrop for Cathy, who sits demurely at his feet with her legs tucked under her, is a wash of greens and yellows, a summery lawn, flat as Omaha, leading up to a large gray house. Both the man and the woman gaze off to their right, as if watching something that he is more engrossed in than she. His expression could be described as "brooding"; hers is merely pleasant, as if she knew her portrait was being painted and wished to look pretty for it. The more I looked at that illustration, the more convinced I became that the artist had no idea what the book was about. Catherine Earnshaw would never sit at anyone's feet. Neither of them would treat the land that held them as a mere backdrop or a view to gaze at. The landscape of Cathy and Heathcliff was no nice lawn; it was the moors, and the humans were incarnate with wild, unimpeded, gale-force winds.

Wuthering Heights is the story of a few thornily interconnected people who inflict love and punishment on one another. The cuts begin when a dour householder brings into his home an orphaned boy named Heathcliff. Catherine, the man's daughter, and Heathcliff form a close bond, while the son, Hindley, resents the interloper. Growing up, Cathy and Heathcliff are rude, daring, careless, and critical of others, but when, as adolescents, they peek into the windows of the upper class manse of Thrushcross Grange, everything changes. Cathy eventually marries the heir, Edgar Linton, and Heathcliff, choked by grief and rage, flees, only to return three years later, with money and determination to wreak revenge. Cathy dies giving birth to a daughter named after her, Heathcliff marries Edgar's sister Isabelle, who bears a child called Linton, and then Heathcliff plots to force the second generation Cathy into a marriage with Hindley's child, Hareton. It all takes place on the Yorkshire moors, whose wind, briars, crags, and desolate expanses chart the fate of the characters and twist their yearnings.

The moors pervade Emily Brontë's one novel. The author does not describe her landscape all at once, as if to position it in the background before concentrating on what another author might consider the more important actions of the characters; she makes the moors a character, too. Rather than writing detailed passages of that land, moreover, she injects frequent, brief encounters between it and the people who abide with it: a lapwing "wheeling over our heads in the middle of the moor," "the wind sounding in the firs," "hazels and stunted oaks." Wuthering Heights, the Earnshaw house, is exposed to the weathers, and "one may guess the power of the north wind, blowing over the edge, by the excessive slant of a few, stunted firs...and by a range of gaunt thorns all stretching their limbs one way, as if craving alms of the sun." "There was no moon, and everything beneath lay in misty darkness." The crags were "bare masses of stone with hardly enough earth in their clefts to nourish a stunted tree." It's as if Brontë was so attuned to this land that she took its presence for granted, even as she marked its temperamental shifts.

In the introduction to the novel Emily's sister Charlotte compared the author herself to a sculptor who, finding "a granite block on a solitary moor," worked it into the shape of a human head. "With time and labour, the crag took human shape; and there it stands colossal, dark, and frowning, half statue, half rock: in the former sense, terrible and goblin-like; in the latter, almost beautiful, for its colouring is of mellow grey, and the moorland moss clothes it." Charlotte, whose own novel, *Jane Eyre*, had been published just two months before *Wuthering Heights*, was calling attention to what readers for a hundred and seventy years have perceived in this rugged, rough-edged book: that it is inseparable from its landscape.

Once, in the middle of perhaps my third reading of *Wuthering Heights*, when I was in my forties, I decided to count the number of scenes that actually take place between Catherine and Heathcliff on the moors. I assumed there would be too many to discern, that the peaks and vales, entrances and exits would roll into one another like the hills themselves. But imagination contrives its own plots. Since the story is told from the point of view of the housekeeper, Nelly Dean, those scenes turn out to be few indeed, and the ones we readers are privy to are but reports and gossip: Catherine recalling how she and Heathcliff dared each other as children to stand in the graveyard and call to the ghosts to come up; Joseph, the gnarly servant, tattling that he's seen the pair up in the moors late at night, even as Cathy is courting Edgar Linton; young Heathcliff explaining why, after a walk with Catherine, he has returned to Wuthering Heights alone. That's about it. In the second half of the book, there's more action on the moors, for Nelly accompanies the overly protected second-generation Cathy on many of her ramblings. I preferred the first part, the first Cathy, even though Brontë's style became more sophisticated as she worked her way through her novel. The Cathy-and-Heathcliff half scraped, bit, screamed, and spat; the second half strolled leisurely. How could a dreamy fifteen-year-old girl, for whom the yearning to escape and the ache to belong were at constant odds, not love a book whose heroine declares, "My love for Heathcliff is like the eternal rocks beneath — a source of little visible delight, but necessary. Nelly, I *am* Heathcliff." For me, the plot, the characters, the setting, and the author herself crystalized all I secretly wrestled with and could never admit.

There was an image I had of myself at that time. No crag of human shape, I felt like a rag doll whose stuffing was coming out at the seams. I hated being that way and wished I could be unruffled and contained, like the popular girls in my class. I had known most of them since I started attending this small private girls' school in seventh grade, after my parents got divorced, and they seemed to have been born into smoothness. Their hair, parted on the side, swung neatly around their chins as they bent over their books in class. Although we wore school uniforms, they had a dress code of their own, which shifted in subtle ways that they either instigated or began following together with the attentive immediacy of pigeons in flight. One year they wore flats and panty hose. For a while they sported circle pins on their blazers. There was a camel hair coat phase, a pink lipstick phase. There was the phase of White Shoulders cologne. No matter what the accouterments, they had a knack for keeping their skirts neat and their white shirts crisp, so they looked the same at the end of the school day as they had when they arrived in the morning. Nothing unpredictable seemed to issue from them. "Oh, God!" they would sigh as they rolled their eyes at one another when something was beneath their consideration.

Even their alarm was calculated. Whenever a bee flew in the classroom window, they would scream and jump out of their seats.

I, to the contrary, got rumpled. My shirt came untucked, ink from my cartridge pen stained my fingers, and my hair was curly and unmanageable. I couldn't keep up with the fashion trends, not only because my mother's job as a secretary at the University of Omaha didn't pay enough to afford such luxuries, but also because I disdained them as much as I coveted them. I longed to be one of the smooth girls and despised the adherence it demanded to their secret rules. I didn't get invited to parties. Often, when I spoke up, the words burst out of me in a sudden gush of revelation, and when that happened, the other girls sighed or pretended not to hear. Every now and then, I tried to imitate them, as if I could act my way into their world. Once, when a bee flew in the window of the biology classroom on a warm spring day, I, too, shrieked and leaped up from my seat. When we all sat back down after a mild chastising by our teacher, I felt a fool.

Restlessness, fury, and desire burned so hot in me that I felt at times it would erupt like a rash on my skin. My parents' divorce had solved one big problem, but I soon found out that it had created others. For years I'd begged my mother to get a divorce. My father was an alcoholic who, when he drank, discovered all kinds of reasons to resent my mother and beat her up for them, and I was the one who had to pull him off, call the police, and wake up my little brother, so we could flee for the rest of the night to a neighbor's house. After the divorce, I had been excited to move with my grandparents into a new apartment, where there was a swimming pool and built-in air conditioning, even though I would now have to share a bedroom with my mother. Shortly after starting at my new school, however, I began to understand class and wealth and how thoroughly they can exclude, for all my classmates had two parents and lived in big homes. Two years after we moved into the apartment, my mother could no longer afford the rent, so, when I was fourteen, we moved into a two-bedroom duplex. Now my brother had his room in the basement, and my mother and I crammed into an even smaller bedroom. She was under the impression that we were both happy with this arrangement. She liked to think of us as best friends, and she often told me that she knew me better than I knew myself. Because she had suffered a lot and was vulnerable, I didn't correct her.

What I was quite sure she had no inkling of were the florid contents of the inner life I was actively conjuring. In the afternoons after school, before my mother got home from work, I would crouch on my bed and peek between the curtains at Johnny Miloni, the handsome law student who lived with his mother in the front part of the duplex, as he shot baskets in the driveway. Johnny was tall and lanky, with black curly hair, and he wore shorts and t-shirts that pulled, when he dribbled and jumped, to reveal olive-colored skin above his shorts. The muscles on his arms rippled when he moved and his skin glistened with sweat. Sometimes I glimpsed his armpits, furred with dark hair. At night, as my mother slept in the twin bed just inches away, I contrived epic fantasies of being swept up in Johnny's arms as he rescued me from tornadoes and school bullies or navigated us to the safety of a desert island after a storm at sea. What I craved was both privacy and liberation. From the library I checked out books about distant places and made detailed itineraries of imaginary journeys that I unfurled on the walk to and from school. That brick house with the circular driveway curving around a garden, for example, was Piccadilly Circus, which I was just now passing on my way to see my publisher about my new book. The intersection of Western Avenue and 60th Street might one day be the gateway to Temple of the Golden Buddha in Bangkok and another day a lane winding through a fishing village in France. After we started reading *Wuthering Heights*, however, all other lands faded. Now it was the moors I crossed to and from school.

Wuthering Heights gave me the inkling that being contained was not so advantageous after all. In fact, studying that book, I encountered not only characters who seemed to have the same kind of unscratchable itch I did, but a new grasp of how an author could throw herself into things like longing, rage, jealousy, and madness as if into a "range of gaunt thorns" and emerge, yes, of course, stung, but with a tale that she had created in the process. The book itself, not the author and certainly not the characters, became the thing contained. The writing had the power to contain all manner of old rags spilling messily out of seams. Without the mess, in fact, the writing could not exist.

As we read the novel, Miss Hansen taught us about the Brontës — the whole family, not just Emily, since you could not talk about one Brontë without talking about all of them. By the time Emily was seven, her mother and two older sisters had died of tuberculosis. Barely four years separated the remaining four siblings, Charlotte, Branwell, Emily, and Anne. The family lived in a two-story building of gray brick at the edge of the village of Haworth in southeastern Yorkshire. Right outside their door rushed the moors. The children's father, Parson Patrick Brontë, was a grim, self-exiled man who preferred to dine alone in his own room. He did have a good library, and he encouraged his children to use it. The young Brontës read eagerly and soon began to create their own imaginary worlds, which they called Angria and Gondol. They wrote the stories of the inhabitants in tiny books they made by cutting pieces of paper into two-inch strips and binding the pages together with thread. Of all the children, tall, thin Emily was the most strong-willed. She refused to attend Sunday school, she was not good at needlework, and she daydreamed. Sometimes she got her way by self-destructive means. At seventeen she enrolled as a pupil at Roe Head School in Mirfield, where Charlotte was working as a teacher, but she was miserable there and, after starving herself for two months, she was sent home. Two years later she herself worked briefly as a teacher in Halifax, eight miles from Haworth, but the work was odious to her, and again she returned to Haworth. As they grew up, the three daughters continued to devote their creative energies to writing, while Branwell became a painter. Emily and Charlotte contrived a plan to start a school of their own and traveled to Brussels to improve their French, but after nine months, they changed their minds. Again the moors and the parsonage took them back. By then, Branwell was in the throes of alcoholism and drug addiction. Charlotte, Emily, and Anne devoted themselves to writing books and in 1847, calling themselves Currer, Ellis, and Acton Bell to disguise the fact that they were women, they sent their three novels to a publisher, who accepted all of them. Emily died a year later, at the age of thirty, of tuberculosis. "We are quite confident that the writer of *Wuthering Heights* wants but the practiced skill to make a great artist," read a review of the book found in Emily's desk after she died.

Emily Brontë's novel is rough. Her writing can be excessively passionate. Even at fifteen I could discern that. But compared to *Wuthering Heights*, other books, both of her time and my own, seemed superficial in their depiction of yearning, an ache that the writers I was familiar with tended to portray as a mild hankering for a sweet, but which, as Emily and I recognized, was actually more like a monster with teeth and claws and a thirst for blood. She knew how to reveal, maybe even revel in, not only cruelty's manifestations, but the drive to commit them. Emily Brontë tortures her characters: a bulldog grabs Cathy's ankle and won't let go, Heathcliff hurls a pot of hot applesauce at taunting Edgar, the narrator of the book scrapes Cathy Linton's wrist back and forth against the jagged edge of a broken window, and Hindley hangs a spaniel by a kerchief on a fence. Love and rage get all tangled up together in this book. One is either proof of the other or a pike right through the middle of it. "Well, if I cannot keep Heathcliff for my friend — if Edgar will be mean and jealous, I'll try to break their hearts by breaking my own," vows Cathy. Did expressing all this violence relieve the author, no stranger to her own brand of self-harm, of a drive for more outward forms of savagery?

In my own life, rage and desire were forces that wracked in ways I would never admit. How could I tell anyone that, even after the divorce, I sometimes still wished my father would die? I'd wither up from shame if anyone found out how, when I watched Johnny Miloni play basketball on the driveway, I wished he would jump, bend, or twist in such a way that I could get a glimpse of the mystery inside his shorts. I knew, too, that I was, to my core, a selfish person. Ever since I was small, my mother had gotten periodic migraines, and when that happened, she had to lie in bed for two or three days with the curtains drawn. In the afternoon, when I got home from school and went into the darkened bedroom, the air smelled of sweaty, stale sweetness. My mother moaned as she greeted me, which I knew was no greeting at all, but a message of her desperation and a plea, aimed at me, for help. "Could you rub my head?" she'd ask. I could. I did. I sat on the edge of the bed beside her and worked my fingers back and forth in her thin, soft hair. Her neck was moist with perspiration, her skull and the pain inside it resisted my hand. In those moments, the prospects for freedom seemed as unreachable as fresh air, untrodden snow, the dunes of the Sahara Desert, a boyfriend, a room of my own. I never could make my mother's headache go away, and I hated both my own powerlessness and her sickness. I hated her for expecting me to make her better, and more than anything I hated myself for so despising this small thing she wanted. So, I punished myself for my wickedness. With my right hand, I kept rubbing gently, just the right pressure she liked, back and forth, back and forth, while at the same time I pressed my left wrist into my mouth and bit down as hard as I could.

In the end, Emily Brontë brings all her characters, with the exception of Nelly Dean, to ruin. She has them torturing one another's psyches until they either die or just manage to hang on, clinging to what we assume will be a life of misery. Even the names of these characters harass and grab: Cathy Earnshaw Linton, Linton Heathcliff, Heathcliff, Hindley Earnshaw, Edgar Linton, Cathy Linton Heathcliff, Hareton Earnshaw — all that C and L and H and E, like cries from hell. What taught this strange, solitary writer so much about passion, cruelty, and suffering? What did she really yearn for? What was it that so enraged her? Whatever it was that got inside her mind and ate away at it like an earwig, she was not afraid to scratch so hard that her very soul poured out into her work. To me, at fifteen, it was all immensely startling and satisfying. *Wuthering Heights* hinted that, one of these days, I would be able to shape my own disorderly outrage and wanting into words.

I had gotten a C on our first essay assignment, a description of my summer vacation. Miss Hansen pointed out that I had written two endings for it and ought to pick just one. However, she had also circled a part of the essay that she liked. The next week, I made sure to write one clear and precise ending, and I studied what I had done in that one paragraph, so I could cadge some style from it. I got an A. And in that moment of looking at the paper she'd handed back and seeing that red mark of excellence inked at the top, something opened up. I got a glimpse of a thing I could do, possibly quite well, and the long path — one whole school year — in which to get better and better at it. In the weeks that followed, I wrote about the Brontës, I wrote a memoir from the point of view of a giant in a laundry soap commercial who lives in the washing machine, about the pop-up place on the outskirts of Omaha that opened only in December to sell Christmas trees, about a statue in front of a Chinese restaurant. After the Beatles came to America, and I fell in love with them, I found a way to write about them a few times. Every week I got an A. An A− was a disappointment. Sometimes I got an A+ and once an A++. On one essay Miss Hansen wrote, "You are becoming one of my favorite writers."

In those essays, I never exposed the details of our embarrassing duplex or my mother sleeping naively in the bed beside mine as I conjured epics that always ended with my being swept up into Johnny Miloni's arms. I didn't write about my own experience with the violence of alcoholism or the torque of envy and contempt I nursed for the girls who never got rumpled. I knew, however, that one of these days, it would be permissible to do so. Emily Brontë and the weekly essays taught me that, no matter how weird or broken your family, or how wild your own cravings, none of it mattered if you could write. That was the great revelation.

Anything at all could be written, and when it was written — or even before that, even while you were in the act of writing it — you had power over the stuff of your life. It could get you down, but it couldn't conquer you.

"Nelly, I *am* Emily!" I practiced the moves of my own possible self each day, autumn, winter, and spring of that year, on my twenty-minute walk to and from school. What united us — Emily, Cathy, and me — was the moors. I walked the straight, flat sidewalks of Omaha as if I were striding over the moors. To walk on the moors was to move with purpose and without restraint. On the moors you could go in any direction. Sidewalks did not limit you, stop signs did not require you to look left and right, people were absent and so did not judge. On the moors you could run away and run toward at the same time. The moors were waves, they were the stratosphere, they were magnets, and they were the physical manifestation of your own inner drive. They were wild, and they wanted to eke the wildness out of you. The moors wanted you out of breath, drenched with the experience of keeping up with their rhythm. And you were glad to comply, because in that breathless state, you were of their making. You were filled with moor and sky, self and purpose, drive and solitude. As I walked each day down the neighborhood streets on my way to school, I was out walking my old idea of myself. The girl with the stuffing seeping from her seams was ripping it all clean out.

I finally visited Haworth Parsonage when I was in my mid-thirties, more than twenty years after we read *Wuthering Heights* in Miss Hansen's class. I went there with the man I would be marrying in a few weeks, along with his son, who was spending his junior year abroad at the University of Edinburgh, and his son's new girlfriend. The Brontës' old home is a large house built of gray stone, not high on a hill like Wuthering Heights, but standing rather snugly at the edge of the village. It's a museum now, with some rooms devoted to exhibitions of Brontë memorabilia and some staged to make it seem that the family still lives there. On the second floor, in one of the bedrooms, a glass case contains the children's tiny books about Angria and Gondol, along with maps and floorplans for those imaginary lands. Downstairs in the dining room, you can stare at the long table where the women wrote their books, as you imagine all the brilliant strokes of the pen that fortunate piece of furniture bore. Near the table stands the black horsehair sofa where Emily died. One of her shawls is draped over the arm. The sofa faces the window and the moors on which Emily must have gazed for sustenance in her last days, even as her body weakened. "I'm sure I should be myself were I once among the heather on those hills," the dying Cathy Earnshaw entreats Nelly. "Open the window again wide: fasten it open!" Next door to the house, the old gravestones in the churchyard heave out of the ground, as if the dead themselves cannot bear their confinement.

When we arrived at the Brontë house, it was late in the afternoon, much later than we had intended. We had gotten delayed in London, and the young people had to be back at the university the following day, so we couldn't stay overnight, as I had hoped. We hurried through the museum and then, because I had expressed my wish to walk on the moors, we all set out together. It was not a gratifying experience. My fantasies of attunement with this landscape had never included others and, to make matters worse, it was apparent that the other three were just indulging me, and their hearts were not in this venture. We strolled, we did not stride. The young woman held back, while father and son kept up a running conversation. I experimented with gunning out ahead of them, but that make-believe rendezvous with my fantasy felt awkward and silly, as unconvincing to the moors as to myself. We turned back after half an hour or so and settled down for tea in one of the shops in town that cater to Brontë tourism, and then we got in the car and headed north. I was excessively disappointed. It wasn't until years later that it occurred to me that I had already made that walk on the Yorkshire moors many times and many years before, when I strode over the moors of Omaha, practicing wildness, freedom, and a writer's life.

DROUGHT

In the summer of 1990, I received a small private grant to spend a month in northeastern Arizona doing research for a book about the Navajo-Hopi land dispute, an issue I had then been covering for more than four years. During that time, I had come to know several people quite well, and my intention was to interweave the points of view of about half a dozen of them to tell the story of the law that was forcing thousands of traditional Navajos off their land, and its complex repercussions. I decided to spend the month filling in the gaps in my knowledge of each person's experience and beginning to braid the stories into a coherent book. Things did not work out the way I'd planned.

In the land "between sacred mountains," where the two distinctly different Hopi and Navajo cultures had lived side by side for more than five hundred years, the Earth was thirsting. The worst fear of Hopi farmers had come to pass: the washes they depended upon to flow down to their cornfields from the forested upland of Black Mesa were dry. Arizonans would remember the summer of 1990 as the hottest and driest in recorded history, but the Hopis blamed the drought not on the weather but on Peabody Coal Company, which pumped a billion and a half gallons of aquifer water a year in order to slurry coal from its strip mine on Hopi and Navajo lands through three hundred miles of pipeline to Nevada. Hopi religious leaders had warned that there would be consequences to pay for the desecration of this sacred female mountain. Now, the mountain was taking its revenge.

Dalton Taylor, a Hopi farmer and member of the Snake Society, who lives in the ancient village of Shungopavi, told me bluntly that no one was going to have time to talk to me. Humans had to perform the tasks the Earth could not. Dalton himself rose before dawn each day to haul buckets of water out to the range where his cattle grazed. After filling the dry, caked catchment pond so the animals could drink, he would crawl under his truck to nap for a spell out of reach of the sun. Nearly every weekend, he attended ceremonies in his own and the other Hopi villages clustered on the edge of three high mesas. From dawn till nightfall, the dusty plazas rang with songs, drums, bells and rattles as the masked kachinas danced their prayers for rain.

The drought was personal as well as meteorological. Although the leaders of both tribal governments had banded together in an effort to urge Peabody to find an alternate means of transporting the coal, relations between Hopi and Navajo families had deteriorated since the passage of the law that was supposed to have settled the land dispute. Clifford Balenquah, a member of the Hopi tribal government, had hoped to build a home on the plateau beneath the mesas, land that had reverted to the Hopis, but his dream, he said bitterly, had proved impossible to realize. Approximately two thousand Navajos who had been ordered to relocate had not only refused to comply with the law, but regularly harassed any Hopi who ventured onto it.

Things were no better among the Navajos whose stories I had hoped to flesh out. Roberta Blackgoat, an elder from the community of Big Mountain, was recuperating from a cataract operation at her daughter's home in Flagstaff. When I first met Roberta in 1986 she had been robust and straight-backed, with a hearty sense of humor. Although the law imposed such severe restrictions on the number of sheep she could have and even the kinds of repairs she could make on her hogan that several members of her family had had to leave the reservation and move to town, she had refused to budge. "My roots go way down deep and can't be pulled out," she'd insisted. Now, sitting on the couch and watching television from behind dark glasses, she had the thin, dry-leaf voice of an old woman, her white hair had lost its sheen, and her face sagged.

I drove over to the winding Ponderosa pine-lined Flagstaff street where Nora Talltree and her family lived.

After years of resisting relocation, the Talltrees had finally concluded that they had no choice but to relocate, even though that meant Nora would be severing the tie to her ancestral land, a bond forged at birth when her father had buried her umbilical cord near the corral. The Talltrees had formed a support group with other relocatees, hoping that, by sharing their experiences, they could ease the pain and isolation that forced relocation invariably brought. But today Nora's skin was sallow and she moved slowly. She told me she had discovered a lump in her breast that tests showed to be malignant. She had had a lumpectomy, followed by two chemotherapy treatments, but the cure made her so sick she had decided to forego modern medical procedures altogether. Now she was seeing an acupuncturist and working with a Navajo medicine man. The medicine man believed the cancer had been caused by spiritual poison, which Nora had absorbed in her long fight against relocation.

After I left Nora's house, I drove to the Museum of Northern Arizona and went out back, where a self-guided trail meanders through high-desert country. It is comforting to walk a path marked by guideposts, but today, I had no sense of where I was headed. Interviewing Nora had made me sick. Over a period of four years I had become familiar with her struggle to fight the law; her worry about her mother, who remained on the land, and her children, who were forgetting their native language; her depression when relatives and neighbors relocated to town and, separated from their land, families, ceremonies, plants, and animals, simply lost the will to live. I had glimpsed her shame after she had done the one thing she vowed she'd never do: taken the government's money for a new house. Today, I had looked down at the tape recorder efficiently soaking up her words and felt I could no longer summon up Nora's or anyone's else's pain for my edification. Still, I had this grant. I had a book to write. I didn't know what I was going to do.

I had started writing about the Navajo-Hopi land dispute because I was appalled that people who knew so well how to live on the land were being forced to leave it. I hoped that by calling attention to what was happening, I might help prevent a cultural crisis with ecological implications, and, at the same time, give people from my own acquisitive, image-conscious white society a glimpse of two peoples who placed supreme value on their relationship with the Earth. My trips to Hopi and

Navajo country were journeys into people's hearts. When I would show up at their door, a white stranger with pads, pen, and a tape recorder, they were wary. At first they would answer my questions in terse, cautious sentences, not wishing to be rude, yet determined to give nothing of themselves away. Then something extraordinary would happen: they began to unfold like a parched plant to the refreshing truth of their own experience. They ceased talking to me and talked simply because there was so much that needed to be told. Sometimes they would catch themselves and ask me not to print something they'd said, but then they would go on as before, the need to speak having grown bigger than the need for discretion.

My own role in this process was not entirely guileless. Although I did not try to incite people to despair, nostalgia, outrage, and fear, I did nothing to stanch such emotions when they arose. I sat quietly, trying to be invisible, the impulse to comfort held in check by my fear that the eloquent passion I was listening to would cease if I called attention to it or to myself, who really had no right to witness it. How these men and women felt when, at last, I drove away and they were left with their emotions spilled all over the place is one of the questions I never asked.

Both I, the interviewer, and those I interviewed behaved as if journalism was the only thing happening between us. I was writing a story, they had information to impart, and for this exchange we had consented to enter into a temporary business partnership. But underneath, each of us longed for something more. Almost everyone I spoke with complained that the true story of the land dispute had never been properly told. What they meant, of course, was that no one had told their truth, and what they hoped was that I would set down accurately not just their words, but their very soul. If that could happen, they believed, the outside world would understand the situation at last and be moved to insist that it be changed. To some that change was repeal of the law, to others it was the eviction of the Navajos, or the banning of industry from Indian land, or the replacement of the white-style tribal councils with traditional leadership — there were countless visions of the ideal future. As for me, I, too, had an idea of how things ought to be different, and it wasn't strictly limited to the land dispute.

"Our life is our religion and our religion is the land," a 21-year-old Navajo man told me once after we had spent the day at Big Mountain and were eating cheeseburgers in a Flagstaff mall. I wished I could say the same. Like a growing number of people, I believed that the only way we could solve our dire environmental problems was to treat the Earth as attentively and considerately as if it were the living, sacred entity indigenous people had always said it was. Or, as the pioneering theologian and ecologist Thomas Berry had written in *The Dream of the Earth*, "The universe itself, but especially the Planet Earth, needs to be experienced as the primary mode of divine presence." I wanted to learn how to listen to the infinite voices of the Earth, how to respect the Earth not just by treading softly upon it, but also by paying homage to it in some way, how to go through the day as if all my tasks were holy.

Over hundreds of years, the Hopi and Navajo people had cultivated ways of living on the land that served them well in both mystical and practical ways. Like most traditional Navajos, Roberta Blackgoat regarded her sheep as a gift from the Holy People. To protect them, she would smoke medicinal plants in a fire and herd the animals through it while she sang prayers. She knew how to care for the sheep when they were sick, how to butcher them for food (after offering some of the blood back to the earth), and how to weave the wool into beautiful rugs with traditional patterns that stylistically depicted the land around Dinetah, the homeland of the Navajo people.

What the nomadic, herding life was to the Navajos agriculture was to the Hopis, descendants of the ancient cliff dwellers. From the time Dalton Taylor had received initiation into the first Hopi religious society as an adolescent boy, he had been learning a complex cosmology in which the universal energies of germination and growth were mirrored in the Hopi cornfields. Throughout the year, he was actively involved in a series of elaborate ceremonies whose purpose was to pray for the well-being of all creatures and, on a microcosmic scale, for rain to nourish the corn that flourished so well in this land of little rain that agriculturalists from all over the world came to study it.

Yankton Sioux author and University of Colorado professor Vine Deloria, whose book, *God is Red*, explores the fundamental differences between the spiritual worldview of Native people and Judeo-Christians, had told me impatiently once when I interviewed him for a magazine article, "You white people need to find your own traditions. They're out there. You don't need ours." But my grandparents had no prayers for the Earth, at least none that they ever taught me. And anyway, it is this land I belong to, this United-States-of-American land, not Sweden or Norway or England, whence my ancestors hailed. Much as I would have loved to learn from them who knew the Earth was alive, they have been dead for millennia and they have left no record of how they worshipped. The Navajo and Hopi people had that direct teaching and, what is more, they practiced it still.

I was not alone in being drawn to their worldview. In the mid-80s, scores of people came to Navajo-Hopi country to volunteer their services on behalf of the Native Americans whom they believed were being victimized by the federal government, energy interests, and their own progressive tribal council leaders. But it was more than a need to right a political injustice that impelled people to leave college, jobs, and families and come out west to work long hours without pay. Saddened by the toxic pall over their cities, the dubious quality of their drinking water, a dwindling number of songbirds in their gardens each spring, and reports of disappearing forests and vanishing species, and feeling powerless to halt the course of destruction, they, too, thirsted for a bond with the natural world that would be more meaningful than simply sorting their recyclable garbage each week.

Therefore, while some sympathizers concentrated on lobbying, fund raising, and doing clerical work in the activist Big Mountain Legal Office in Flagstaff, others had determined that their services must consist of nothing less than going up to the land to live with Navajo elders and help them with chores, while absorbing their way of life. The Navajos accepted with grace as much as gratitude, joking privately about volunteers who panicked when a sheep started giving birth or who fled for home with a heavy stomach after a steady Navajo diet of mutton, fry bread, and strong coffee laced with sugar. Ivan Sidney, the Hopi tribal council chairman from 1982 to 1990, was convinced that non-Indian volunteers were inciting the Navajos to disobey the law by staying on the land. Noting that some of them sported Indian-style windbands and beaded jewelry, and adopted names like Swaneagle and Little Bear, he condemned them as "Wannabe's." They insisted, however, that they did not "wanna be" Indian. "These old women are completely different from the grandmothers in our white society," said a young German woman, who had spent several weeks with one of the elders of Big Mountain. "They stand against the BIA [Bureau of Indian Affairs], the police, against relocation, against the policies of the energy companies. These women are living there with the Earth. They are bonded with the animals, the plants, the mountains. Their lives have become real hard. I came to help them and to get an education from them."

I felt the same way. I, too, wanted to get an education from the Navajo and Hopi, elders and youth alike. And my secret hope was that Americans who read the articles and books by me and other journalists would be so moved by the stories of the people that they would both demand that the law be amended and revise their thinking about their own place on the Earth.

By the summer of 1990, the activist energy that had powered all sides of the issue in 1986 had sputtered like the engine of an old pickup. The law was still in effect, there were still Navajos living on the land that had been partitioned to the Hopis, and relocation was still destroying individual lives and ancient traditions. But the volunteers had drifted on to other causes. Reporters and photographers who had covered the issue amidst rumors that the National Guard might be summoned to haul elderly sheepherders off the land on the day of the federal relocation deadline in July 1986 had lost interest once the colorful footage had faded into black-and-white stills of exhausted people waiting for change. Maybe the oppressive heat made things worse, but it seemed to me that both peoples just wanted to be left alone to carry on their lives. The imperatives of getting water to the cattle and regaining personal health had forced them to shift their attention away from the endless problem of the land dispute and concentrate instead on raw physical survival. This may even have been a relief. At any rate, Dalton Taylor was right: most people were unable or unwilling to talk to me about the land dispute, an issue that had become as oppressive, stagnant, and impervious to human will as the relentless hot weather. I had to wonder if my own reluctance to dredge up their pain might not also be responsible in some karmic way for the swath of missed appointments and excuses I kept encountering.

And so, for the first time since I'd been traveling in Hopi-Navajo country, I had free time. One thing I did was explore the land. No matter where you stand on the land between sacred mountains, you comprehend, on a visceral rather than an intellectual level, how the myths about the place arose and why the indigenous people consider it sacred. On previous trips I had rarely ventured beyond the driver's seat of my rental car, as I covered the miles from one hogan, one Hopi village, to another, packing in as many interviews as I could. Now I hiked in the San Francisco Peaks and Oak Creek Canyon, tracked wild elk across the undulating grassland of Garland Prairie, visited Anasazi sites, and joined a local botanist on a trek to identify medicinal plants. One day Nora Talltree took me to Blue Canyon, where she had grown up. She and her daughter Amy and I sat in one spot, midway between the flat, treeless land above the earth and the canyon floor below, and Nora told stories. She told about the holy Changing Woman, who walks the length of the canyon to collect offerings people leave for her; about Navajo families who made their homes at the foot of those tall red cliffs and whose ways were so traditional that they still got around by horse and wagon; about the blue-green clay her mother had scooped from the earth and molded into people and animals for the children to play with; about the time some herders had seen a spaceship land on a flat grassy area that was so marked by the phenomenon that nothing had grown there since; about the days she and her sisters had spent here herding sheep and exploring the recesses, niches and furbelows in the rock; and about an ancient shrine where they had found brilliant parrot feathers and the charred remains of an offering of corn. I realized sadly that non-indigenous Americans could never reach such a profound multi-dimensional experience of a place. Even those who have lived on a farm for many generations and who have acquired both knowledge of and love for the land, have no creation myths or stories of epic events to suffuse local land forms with numinous energy. Moreover, although I was convinced that many non-Indians had experienced mysterious and heartfelt interactions with animals, plants, soil and rivers, they rarely spoke of them, perhaps thinking them either figments of their imagination or a sign of mental instability.

Besides exploring the land, I did what I could to be of use. I brought groceries to Roberta Blackgoat at her daughter's house and stayed to watch a video of "The Bear" with Roberta and her two little great-granddaughters; drove a Hopi elder around the BIA's official labyrinth so he could get information about the use of Hopi water by outside interests; and spent weekends attending ceremonies on the Hopi mesas. I was surprised how hard it was at first to tuck in my journalistic antennae, always buzzing to pick up clues, and to quit trying to be invisible.

One night, a friend of mine, a former easterner who had moved to Flagstaff after a single visit to the Grand Canyon, listened while I tried to unravel the problem of whether whites desperate for an Earth-based spirituality were violating native people by trying to imbibe theirs. "Our ancestors knew the Earth was sacred, too," she said, and got up to search her bookcase. That night in the little one-room cabin I had rented for the month, I started reading *The Death of Nature: Women, Ecology and the Scientific Revolution* by Carolyn Merchant. Merchant traces European attitudes toward the natural world from the Middle Ages and Renaissance, when the whole Earth was conceived as a living female body, fecund and mysterious, to the late 17th century, when the invention of earth-moving forges, windmills, and pumps encouraged the view that nature was a mechanism that could not only be understood but controlled. I was amazed to learn that it had not been millennia, as I had assumed, but only a few hundred years, since a divine presence had been as immanent in the forests and fields of Europe as it was today in the land between sacred mountains. For example, the popular Renaissance image of the Earth's anatomy, in which ore flowed through her subterranean veins, gold germinated in her womb, and gases built up pressure in her bowels until they burst as earthquakes, made me think of Roberta Blackgoat's designation of Black Mesa, where the coal was being mined, as the liver of Mother Earth. Paracelsus, the 16th century Swiss physician and alchemist, taught that every facet of the cosmos was imbued with astral spirit, a substance that came originally from the stars and provided humans with a direct and conscious link to the divine plan. This sense of the ongoing viability of the germ of creation was similar to the Hopi belief that every ceremony literally re-enacted and renewed the universal creative process. And the Hopi and Navajo view that all aspects of nature are brothers and sisters whose life profoundly affects every other earthly being, had a counterpart in the theory of Vitalism put forth by Anne Conway, a seventeenth century Englishwoman, who tried to combat the emerging mechanistic worldview by arguing that each creature had a "central or governing spirit" and that all beings "mutually subsist one by another, so that one cannot live without another."

It is true, unfortunately, that by the time Bernardino Telesio of Italy was writing that God was omnipresent in nature and that all matter was alive, his late countryman, Christopher Columbus, had enslaved the Arawak peoples of the Caribbean and forced them to desecrate their sacred mountains to supply him with gold. Moreover, even the pantheistic theories of the Europeans were filtered through the fundamental tenets of Judeo-Christian monotheism, so they reflected the assumption of human superiority set forth in Genesis, when God cast Eve and Adam out of Eden, exhorting them to have dominion over "the fish of the sea, over the birds of the air, and every living thing that moves on the Earth." For instance, in Conway's metaphysics, there was a hierarchical chain of being in the universe, in which each entity, from dust to humans, could attain increasingly high levels of perfection. This glorification of progress runs counter to the indigenous view that each being already perfectly fulfills its role in the cosmic web of life. Still, I was delighted to know that, not so long ago, my ancestors had regarded trees and rivers as entities imbued with spirit. It put me in closer relation to their ancestors, tribal people who had danced around sacred fires to propitiate the deities of thunder and lightning, who had followed strict codes of behavior when the imminence of the harvest or the hunt meant life or death for the community, who had prayed for guidance from birds and animals — and received it.

Not long after I began to hear the echo of my ancestors' footsteps on the earth, a Hopi friend who knew of my fondness for sleeping outside, gave me directions to a canyon north of Oraibi, on land where his family had grazed their cattle since his grandmother's day. The canyon was a long narrow rip of earth that zigzagged farther to the west than I felt inclined to follow (although I wondered if it might eventually link up with Nora's Blue Canyon) and was about as wide as a New York City street. The sand at the bottom was soft and white and held the prints of coyotes and snakes. In places the rock walls, colored like bread, blood, and honey, had tumbled down on top of one another. Juniper and piñon trees had improbably taken root among them, and thrust out over the space below like the necks of curious mountain goats. Nothing of the world beyond the rim was visible except turquoise sky. As the turquoise faded to pale blue, then gray, swallows darted through the channel of sky on last important errands. Then a great emptying took place — of light, warmth, flight, color, sound — and finally the stars began to emerge. Slowly, the moon, a couple of days past full, made its way through the boughs of a juniper tree, cleared it, and shone down. I did a dance of gratitude to the place for allowing me to see its beauty, and then I wriggled into my sleeping bag on the sand.

When I woke the moon had arced high above the canyon. Its light silvered the sand and the tips of yucca blades on the rim, and showed darkness pooled in the hollows of the rocks. Inches above my head, a cricket sang. Cradled in the canyon, I felt the abounding presence of many forces of nature, including those I could not see, like the cricket, or even hear, like the animals stepping softly, searching for food, and the physical forces that whirled in the rocks, holding them up or urging them to let go and plunge. Overhead the stars slowly revolved, predictable and incomprehensible. And at that moment I knew nothing so well as how the first humans who woke to consciousness and stood shivering before the mystery of life had recognized the Earth as their original and most divine mother.

Before dawn, when night was still thick in the west, and the sky a starless charcoal smudge in the east, I crawled up out of the canyon on all fours and sat on a rock to await the sun. It was a long wait, the modulations of light so subtle as to be almost unnoticeable. At one moment I was seized with panic that this might be the one day in four and a half billion years when the sun would not appear. When the first rays pierced the brightening haze over the horizon I was exhilarated. Now the sun was no enforcer of drought but the giver of radiant life after the night that was gestation in the womb of the Earth.

I ended up writing a book that focused on how the Navajo and Hopi people had used their wit and passion and ingenuity over the years to cope with the so-called "settlement" of the land dispute. It was never published. Whether the articles and the radio documentary I wrote over the years and the talks I gave benefited the people they concerned I do not know; I fear that they did not. I'm sure I gained far more from the people on the land between sacred mountains than I was able to give.

From the Hopi and Navajo people I learned a great deal about how spiritual theories and practical tasks are indivisible when you enact them in a sacred place, permeated with abundant, vital energy. I also saw how even that potent energy, which has accrued over hundreds of generations of conscious interaction between people and nature, can be extinguished when federal laws restrict such simple traditional practices as building a hogan or when industries use abundant stores of water while ancient cornfields wither. Over four years, I was honored to attend ceremonies vastly older than any Christian or Jewish rite ever celebrated on this continent, to visit sacred places and hear stories of their origin, to eat meals by lamplight, and sleep in a hogan on a pile of sheepskins, and to hear in countless eloquent ways how people love and take care of the land that has taken care of them.

But the details of Navajo and Hopi life were not what influenced my own behavior toward the Earth. I do not say Hopi and Navajo prayers or enact Hopi and Navajo ceremonies, and I have not transplanted Hopi and Navajo cosmology to northeastern Pennsylvania, where I live with my husband. Rather, I gained from the people I met the faith that nature is alive, and that it communicates to anyone who acts respectfully toward it and is willing to listen to it. I understand now that, although we non-Indians lack a mythology of our place on this continent, we still have access to the land's unique energy, including most especially the land where we live. On my own land, for example, I can make it a point to learn the age of the rocks, the quality of the soil and the special properties of the plants, so that rocks and plants and soil become as co-inhabitants of the place, with needs and habits and propensities. I can imagine as I walk in the woods behind my house the footsteps of the animals and the indigenous people who preceded me. And I can note the sites where significant events occur on the land — not just natural events, but also those that lace together the human spirit and the spirit of the place: from the dead poplar branch in the pond where a blue heron perched to scan the water for frogs, to the patch in the shade of the house where the last of the snow melts in spring, to a place in the meadow where a friend played her cello one gray autumn Saturday. All this knowledge and imagination — all this attention — becomes the point on which the land's sacredness pivots, for these places become more fully enriched with meaning every time I recollect the events that happened there and share them with others. I am deepening the roots so that, as Roberta Blackgoat would say, "they can't be pulled out."

THE JUNIPER TREE

We got out of the car at a bend in the road of the mountain the Dineh (Navajo) call *TsoodziL*, Blue Bead or Turquoise Mountain, the sacred mountain of the south. We were two Anglos from New York, photographer Karen Marshall and I, and for a few years each of us had been covering a federal law that was displacing thousands of the most traditional indigenous people in the land now called Arizona. This was the first time Karen and I had worked together, and we were collaborating on a feature story. For a few days we had been interviewing people in their hogans and in a café in Window Rock and had received permission from Dineh friends to drive up the mountain and take photos. As soon as we stopped, Karen started gathering her equipment.

Oddly, I felt another pull. "I think I'm going to walk back that way," I told her, indicating the empty road we'd driven down.

I walked, not with purpose, but not aimlessly either. I walked as if my feet were remembering something my brain had long forgotten or as if a tune were playing to a part of my body in frequencies too low for my ears to hear. Just a few yards from the car I started climbing up a slope heavily forested in juniper and pinyon trees, the ones Dineh Roberta Blackgoat called "the two sisters," since the juniper's long tap root and the pinyon's massive system of shallow roots enables them to live side by side without competing for water.

At one large juniper I stopped. I was close enough to the road that I could spot the car through the branches of the trees. Karen would have heard me if I'd called out to her. I stopped there, because it seemed that was what was expected of me. The tree was ancient. If three people had been able to crouch down under its low, outflung branches, they would not have been able to clasp hands around the trunk. The bark was silver, shaggy, and soft to the touch. I had only been standing there for a moment when something started happening to my body. I felt love seeping up from the ground and into my feet and then slowly rising through my legs, torso, arms, neck, head. It wasn't heat I felt, not tingling, certainly nothing I could have identified as a physical sensation. It was love, and it was coming not from me but towards me, into me. There is no other way to say this: it was love, it was coming from a juniper tree, and it was filling me up. For a few seconds, probably less than a minute, my entire body bathed in it. Then, as slowly as it had arisen, it started emptying out and down, head to feet. And then it was gone.

Shaken with awe, I stayed with the tree for a few minutes more, holding my hands against its furry bark, moving my face against its lacy needles. I could not imagine any possible way to express my gratitude. Then I turned around and went down the hill.

Karen was crouched on the side of the road, photographing the valley below. She glanced at me. "Something happened to you up there," she said. "I'm not going to ask what it was."

Not only did I not tell Karen about it, I've told few others. Stories about events that lack logical explanations make a lot of people uncomfortable, and when I have dared to relate such things, the rationales or embarrassed silence that often follows makes *me* uncomfortable. Nevertheless, ever since I was a little girl, that's the world I've wanted to get intimate with. There is an Inuit song that begins, "In the very earliest time, / when both people and animals lived on earth.... All spoke the same language. / That was when words were like magic."

I longed to slip into that magical place where everything speaks the same language. I wanted to understand what the birds were saying, to know what it felt like to be the willow tree in my back yard, to grasp the society of the tiny lives that wriggled in a rain puddle. I didn't want to *find* the Source so much as I wanted to lose the humanness that separated me from it. And occasionally that's happened. For instance, I received love from a juniper tree. Once, when I was picking my way down a rocky slope in the Sahara Desert of southern Algeria, a raven flew up from behind me, and for a few seconds I was lofted up into the bird's point of view, not human anymore, without memory or even wonder, just a flying being who noted with interest the Tuareg guides in their bright cotton gandoras, making lunch in the valley below. Once at a Shoshone ceremony I was so possessed by ecstasy that I started spinning and screeching all around the room.

Here's what I'm sure of: each of those encounters really did happen. I know they happened not only because I experienced them once, but also because whenever I think of them, awe sizzles through me. What I'm not sure about, what I ask myself over and over is: Who gets to have meetings with Mystery? Did I do something right and good to earn those experiences? Or were they due to some chemical phenomenon that catalyzed when two normally separate energies crossed and sparked? Was there a scientific reason for what happened or was it spiritual — and could it be both at once?

In his book, *Beyond Words*, Carl Safina recounts the story of a herder who was struck by the trunk of an aggressive African elephant matriarch. The blow so injured the man's leg that he was unable to walk. The elephant, apparently realizing his plight, used her trunk to move him under the shade of a tree, then she stayed with him throughout the night, occasionally touching him with her trunk. Did the elephant feel responsible for the man's condition? Did she regret her action? Had the herder done something to deserve the blow — or was he more deserving of the extraordinary caretaking he later received?

Stories like this, in which humans and other beings share a moment of profound and ineffable connection, are becoming more than anecdotal as scientists investigate the inner lives of animals. For example, in an article about intuitive interspecies communication (IIC) for *A Research Agenda for Animal Geographies*, the authors describe their "methodological and political venture that…. challenges (and invites) researchers and learners of the method to understand and engage with animals as social peers, communicative partners and co-researchers." One of the authors, Viktoria Hinz, intends to pursue this field so she can work with wildlife, rather than managing it, to learn from the animals themselves the best ways of protecting their habitats.

Both the stories and the research convince me that animals can communicate to humans their needs, their pasts, their displeasure, and their affection. But can we also share emotions with trees, rivers, or mountains? With her studies of the complex networks by which trees warn one another of disease and protect young saplings, Suzanne Simard has shown that a forest is as abuzz with shared requests and responses as an old office switchboard. That chemistry in fungi and roots catalyzes the interactions among plants has gained widespread acceptance, even among former skeptics, though many still sneer at the belief, common among plant lovers, that houseplants thrive best when they're treated to classical music and loving attention. Masaru Enomoto believed that water has similar reactions to kindly offerings. In a series of famous, critically challenged, experiments, he photographed droplets of polluted water under a microscope, then focused words like "love" and "peace" on droplets from the same source before photographing them. The water in the "before" pictures look like lumpen blobs; the "after" water drops are intricate, beautiful crystals.

Even rock speaks to and quivers with its environment. In 2018 scientists attached seismic recording equipment to Castleton Tower, a stately formation of redrock presiding over the Utah desert. The rock, they discovered, hums in a low and varying tone that sounds like a cross between a whale's song and the drone of a jetliner. Every now and then the tone skips or wavers, as if something has happened to it. And, yes, something has happened. Castleton Tower, which vibrates at about the same frequency as a human heartbeat, is responding to wind, distant tremors in the earth, heat and cold, and passing cars. "We like to think of it as a voice," said Dr. Jeff Moore, one of the geologists who is monitoring that and other rock formations. "It's sort of alive with this vibrational energy."

I feel comforted and encouraged when I read that there is scientific proof that trees help one another, that rocks note the motorized traffic of humans, and elephants feel something like regret. These studies affirm that the whole Earth is alive, and each entity in its own way is intelligent and reactive to its environment. Science can now explain the reasons for things like volcanoes and eclipses that our ancestors considered manifestations of the pleasure or displeasure of the gods. Knowing the science behind cosmic phenomena doesn't make them less wondrous, it only opens the possibility of more wonders. It also unites the realms of spirituality and science, all too often presumed to be in conflict. One day, perhaps, Emoto's theories will be vindicated by science, just as Galileo's were. For now, we can still ponder: Can a tree give love? Can a human being really be snatched up into the consciousness of a raven? Does everything, including rocks, have a soul?

Once I read an article in *Parabola* Magazine by a doctor, Christian Wertenbaker, who was trying to figure out the composition of the soul. In order to be compatible with a scientific worldview, he wrote, the soul must be assumed to have certain properties, such as being able to maintain its integrity for a long time, "perhaps forever", and possessing a consciousness of the world and the ability to act on it. The soul, he proposed, might be made of plasma. To many the idea would sound extraordinary. Maybe one day we'll find out he was right. Would that knowledge render the soul, whether you view it as the force that reincarnates after death, joins God in heaven, or guides us to our highest purpose in life, any less marvelous? Would receiving love from a tree or flying with a raven be less extraordinary if I were to learn that those beings and I were on the same vibrational frequencies? I don't think so. I think I would be more, rather than less, affirmed in my belief in the spiritual maxim that all things in the universe belong to the same family, that, really, we do speak the same magic language. And if I were to learn that these mysteries landed in me solely because I was somehow spiritually worthy, I would try to develop the appropriate actions with which to respond. In either case I would be, and am, profoundly grateful.

DEVOTING

My friend, the late Agung Detra Rangki, Balinese Hindu, scholar of his religion and culture, told me once, when I had not seen him for a while and asked what he'd been doing, that he had been "how would you say — devoting." He meant that he had been spending time with his spiritual devotions. In Bali this means making offerings, praying to the gods, participating in the ceremonies in his village. The word struck me. My deepest longing, since I was a small child, had been to be in the presence of the potent, conscious force that I was convinced animated the cosmos. Agung's poetic description of his own practice made me realize that I, too, had been "devoting" for many years. And what I have devoted myself to is the search for the force that impels faith. This is my spiritual practice and ongoing query.

Yet, here's a confession: my devoting follows not one path, but many. I've never lived in an ashram or considered entering a convent. I never looked into the gaze of a teacher and knew I was being called to be that one's disciple. I am very bad at meditating. I have joined in the prayers of many faiths and felt them to be moving, genuine, and indisputably aimed right toward — and quite conceivably heard by — that which people call "God," yet I have never been tempted to convert. I've had no interest in finding the one spiritual home I would never have to leave. What I've longed for instead is to experience the divine as it manifests in the world. And since every faith defines a path to God, and many secular actions crisscross those spiritual paths, I've chosen to partake of a variety of practices and, most important of all, to stay on the lookout for evidence of the Great Mystery moving through life.

This approach to spiritual practice is not recommended, I know. Often I have come across stern pronouncements directed at people like me: One cannot dabble, say the priests and scholars. Spirituality is not a tasting menu. "New Agers" who borrow a bit of this religion and a bit of that, while discarding the parts they don't like, will never have anything but a shallow and delusional relationship with the sacred, they warn. Respectfully, I disagree. Seeking itself can be a practice. And what I have discovered, over and over again, is that the more open I am to finding the holy in any place, time, or circumstance, the more likely I am to be invited into a brief encounter with it.

Accompanying a dozen African-American ministers from around the U.S., I take a "toxic tour" of four communities along the Mississippi River near New Orleans. Two towns are squeezed up against petrochemical industries so gargantuan, noisy, fiercely-lit, and foul-smelling that garden flowers die and children can't play outside. Another has a landfill for its next-door neighbor. The fourth place bears a story not only of disrespect and toxicity, but of insidious cruelty. After friends and families received land and low-interest mortgages with which to build a new community, they discovered that their dream village sits right on top of a toxic landfill. The people in all these communities are fighting for justice, but they often feel no one is paying attention. The visit from the ministers renews their hope. At every stop we make we meet people who tell their stories, and then the church women welcome the delegation with a feast of fried chicken, greens, mashed potatoes, rolls, and pie. Before eating, we bow our heads as the ministers call the attention of the Lord to the predicament at hand. "The gates of Shell are the gates of hell," bellows one reverend. "Ay-men," choruses the group. The prayers are powerful, but the true act of grace is the outpouring of hospitality and generosity offered by people facing such calamities.

Night has long since fallen over the mosque in this residential section of Istanbul when the rustle of settling-in fades and a dozen men in long robes step into the round, wood-paneled room. One by one they bow to the sheik, remove their robes, unfurl their arms like petals, and begin to spin. In the ceremony of sema, *members of the Order of the Whirling Dervishes mirror with their bodies the movement of the universe, from the spinning of planets around the sun to electrons circling their nucleus. Left arm angled down to the earth, right arm up toward God, each man spins in his own circle, while all orbit together around the space. The heavy hems of their white robes undulate like waves. Part human, part divine, part cosmic force, they spiral straight to God.*

Witnessing, yet separate from, the vast realms they pass through, I ache to be a passenger on their journey.

And why should we not partake of the wisdom of other paths, not just as observers, but, to the extent that we're able, as participants? Ever since the late nineteenth century, when spiritual leaders like Japanese Zen Buddhist monk Soyen Shaku and Hindu Swami Vivekananda of India came to the United States to offer their teachings to westerners, opportunities to learn spiritual practices from around the world have increased. Countless books, articles, and now the internet offer a wide, clear, sparkling stream of insight and information to those longing to be schooled in unfamiliar, yet alluring paths to the divine. Of course there are cautions. Some Native Americans have objected strenuously to non-Natives borrowing traditions like the sweat lodge ceremony, especially since such actions seem a perpetuation of the centuries-old habit of colonizers helping themselves to that which belongs to indigenous people. But I would say that most of the "devoting" of eclectic mystics like me is less about absconding with the ceremonies of others than imbibing vital wisdom that can guide us in shaping our lives. And of course whenever I do receive an invitation into the spiritual heart of another tradition, I cannot but say, wholeheartedly, *yes.*

The medicine man from this western tribe and his assistants are dressed in full ceremonial regalia: buffalo headdress, feathers, beaded deerskin boots. Slowly they turn to face the night in each of the four directions, blow on their eagle-bone whistles, shake their rattles, and call in the spirits. We, the participants, turn too, hushed, anticipating this ceremony that is said to be more than a thousand years old. And as those ancient calls go out, I feel presences sweeping in like banners of silk. I feel their curiosity. I can tell, without quite seeing them directly, that women are here, and men, and even several children. They have returned. Awe puckers the flesh on my arms. The world beyond the world is real, there are those who know how to open the door and call it over to the place where we normally live, and when the beings of that world are called, they may just come.

I could say I learned certain lessons from such moments of grace, moments of witness, moments of the parting of the veil, but that isn't quite right. These experiences were like benign electrocution; they flashed through me, body and soul, and seared my nerve endings, permanently altering how I perceived and received the world. Each experience remains an image bathed in a truth. As William James points out, one of the most significant aspects of the mystical experience is its "noetic quality":

> Mystical states seem to those who experience them to be also states of knowledge. They are states of insight into depths of truth unplumbed by the discursive intellect. They are illuminations, revelations, full of significance and importance, all inarticulate though they remain; and as a rule they carry with them a curious sense of authority for after-time.

I'm not saying that experiences like praying before a meal offered by generous people in dire straits count as a "mystical states." Still, they are openings of the way, moments of weighty truth. They are epiphanies, and they often arise in times and places outside the bounds of spiritual tradition. They can make you see the world, and your part in it, anew

In a subway station in New York City I watch as a disheveled, dirty man, who has been leaning against the wall, sinks slowly to the floor. I notice, but I do not move from my spot on the platform, where I am positioned to push quickly into the train. What do I assume about this man? That he is drunk? Homeless? Exhausted? That the condition he's now in, while not exactly normal, could not possibly be a real emergency? One young woman in the crowd of commuters, perhaps on her way to college or her first job, walks briskly over to the man. She bends over him, touches his shoulder, asks if he's all right and if he needs help. There is nothing — not sickness, fear, filth, embarrassment, or a time schedule — that she will permit to separate her from what she is called to do right now. Around these two souls radiates the glow of mercy.

For eight years I lead a contemplative journey and camel caravan in the Sahara desert. My Swiss co-guide, our participants, and I are in turn guided by a band of Tuareg, a nomadic, musical, matriarchal culture and the indigenous people of the region. For several days we ride camels through the desert, stopping at night to sleep under the stars. We then settle for a week in one spot, where the participants go on a three-day solo. This year we're camped in a sandy valley, on either side of which escarpments of black, tumbled rock lead up to a stony plateau. On the third day of the solo my co-guide, our assistant, and I are sitting and talking on the rocks about two hundred feet above the valley. Down below, our Tuareg hosts sprawl on mats talking and laughing as the cook stirs a pot on a small fire. Then the camel master waves his arms up to us to indicate that lunch is ready, and we start heading down, each picking our own way among the boulders. Behind me I hear the thwack-thwack of heavy wings and look up to see a raven. Suddenly, inexplicably but surely, my consciousness ceases to belong to me and I am seeing the valley from the bird's perspective. I see my friends far below, moving among rocks; the Tuareg in their colorful robes like miniature action figures left outside by a child; the camel saddles, like charms on a bracelet, spread out on the sand. I am flying high over the valley, and then, suddenly, I reach the plateau and land with a jolt back in my own body, negotiating the rocks as the bird flies on. Stunned, I tell no one, though I wonder over this flight every day.

That which stretches beyond and beneath the known, that which moves the world, from consciousness to quarks, that which impelled the universe into being and drives it still, that Great Mystery that seduces humans to seek it out, though they are permitted to find it only in the tiniest of glimpses — that wondrousness goes by many names. It also possesses many qualities, even when it is the Tao and its attributes include having no attributes at all. It is loving, it is vengeful and demanding, it is billions of years of nature becoming increasingly conscious. It is the unified field that holds the universe together. It wants you to be good, so your life after death will be paradisal, and it has no interest in you at all. Even those who don't believe in it occasionally experience it. It is the Unknown we yearn to know more of.

Eliezer Shore writes that, according to Hasidic texts, although the soul is focused in the body, it doesn't end there. It can be found in our belongings, in places and even things that have not yet found their way into our lives. Thus, "all of life is a gathering up of soul." My own spiritual practice has been a quest to gather up the parts of my soul in order to gain a closer relationship with the Great Unknown. I have found pieces of my soul in places where I deliberately went looking and in utterly unexpected places. What has drawn many of them forth, I believe, is simply that I am always on the lookout for them.

In December 2009 I attended the Parliament of the World's Religions in Melbourne, Australia. The theme was "Hearing Each Other, Healing the Earth," and the focus was the imperative for the spiritual traditions of the world to devote more of their liturgy, teaching, and outreach to addressing ecological challenges. Throughout the week, in hundreds of panel discussions, talks, workshops, and offerings of music and dance, leaders in many spiritual traditions created a living mandala around this theme, as complex and colorful as the sand mandala slowly blossoming under the tools and attention of Tibetan Buddhist monks. On the last day of the parliament His Holiness the Dalai Lama was scheduled to speak. That morning everyone had to pass through metal detectors to enter the Convention Center. Then we had a lengthy wait in the lobby outside the auditorium, thousands of people ranging in long messy lines that kept diverging and merging as conversations arose. Finally the doors were opened.

And we were rushing in. Christians, Aboriginals, Muslim women in jilbabs, Sikhs in white turbans, Yoruba in colorful robes, Tibetan Buddhists in saffron, Jews, Samis, Buddhists, Navajos, Pagans, Hindus, Ainu, Jains: we were all surging through the doors and dashing toward the front of the auditorium. I had not been in such a fervent charge for the stage since I saw the Beatles perform live. Here there was no pushing, no shoving, no shouting; this was not Black Friday at Wal-mart. However, we all knew we were about to be in the presence of exceptional enlightenment, and we wanted to snag the best seat possible. I had the sense that this great tide we were creating together mirrored both the general impulse for attendance at the parliament and the course our individual lives had taken. For although there are many names for God, many paths for seeking and practicing union with the divine, and, all too often, many injurious ways of asserting the supremacy of one's own faith — when it comes right down to it, we are all dashing exuberantly towards the holy.

PART III
Love And Grief

DRUNK WITH VIRTUE

My mother always said a nice girl never lets a boy know how much she likes him. I trusted my mother, so I settled early into the rigors of loving in secret.

When I was eight, I fell in love for the first time. He was Hal Stalmaster, the boy who played Johnny Tremaine in the Walt Disney movie. Each time I asked for money to see it again, I lied and said I liked the silversmithing scenes.

When I was thirteen, I would lock myself in my room and peer through a slit in the curtains as the handsome law school student next door practiced shooting basketballs through a hoop. In all these years I have never sat through a basketball game, but I recall vividly the sensual athletics of Johnny Miloni dribbling and concentrating, twisting his hips and dancing his long, tan, bare arms. As he slam-dunked, his feet left the ground, his head tilted back, his hand touched the hoop, and his shoulder muscles pulled at the back of his white T-shirt. When the ball went in, I witnessed a combination of physical beauty and athletic prowess that would have rendered me incapable of speech had anyone made a sudden entrance into my bedroom. If I heard footsteps coming down the hall, I bolted back from the window, so no one would guess the desire I was up to.

I discovered that there are advantages to loving in secret. First of all, you're in control: your love is like one of those magic rings in fairy tales that only the wearer can remove. Your beloved can break you heart over and over again with his indifference, but because your passion thrives on elaborate, unshared dreams, he can never make you give up hope. Moreover, loving in secret makes you powerful. Because the rest of the world is ignorant of your secret, it will see moments between the two of you, if it sees them at all, as flat and simple. You, however, are aware that every encounter is dense with fate and symbolism .

In high school I had a crush on my best friend's brother, and not even she guessed my secret until I revealed it in my first book. Other girls in my class would giggle and conspire together over boys who were cute, boys who had a good personality, boys they'd kissed, and boys they'd impressed with a smart retort, boys they hoped would call. I envied their immodesty, and it appalled me. Nothing could have persuaded me to air my love so frivolously.

After I discovered the Beatles and became infatuated with Paul, I'd lie awake each night long after switching off the bedside lamp, just for the pleasure of plotting the next episode in my mental love epic. I dreamed up scenes in which my famous boyfriend loved and rescued and adored me. However, just to be on the safe side, I kept even my fantasies chaste, for I suspected that if a girl admitted her true feelings for a boy, she would be dangerously close to committing that other, ultimate act of sordid behavior my mother had told me a nice girl had to guard against before she was married.

The way I envisioned it, therefore, romance took place in vaporous landscapes involving a river, mist, and willow trees. He and I would share profound respect. He would save me from endless tribulations — tornadoes, shipwrecks, crude men who wanted only one thing from me — and I, the only person who understood him, would soothe his sweet, soulful pain. We would never speak of the love that was unfolding between us. I was too well trained for such indelicacy, and he, out of respect, never embarrassed me by blurting out a confession of his own. Then one day he would present me with an engagement ring and, I, trembling with relieved joy, would accept.

Even though my mother didn't like to talk about sex, she did have a point of view about it. She said that if you were married to the right man, it could be very beautiful. This assertion saddened me, for I knew she could not have made it from personal experience. My mother had not married the right man. My father, a stranger with a briefcase and a black Plymouth, was often away on business trips. When he came home, he drank gin, blackened my mother's eyes and broke her nose, and cleared shelves with the back of his hand. We fled across the dark suburban lawns to sanctuary at neighbors' houses, and in the morning, coming home to get ready for school, we stepped over him, passed out in his underwear at the foot of the stairs or in the front seat of the car. They finally divorced when I was twelve. In the first few years of her new singleness, my mother dated several men, but she never went out with the same man more than two or three times. Years later, I came to believe it was because she still considered herself a nice girl and would not grant the favors of a married woman.

My mother's belief in the virtue of restraint extended to domains other than the sexual. She believed in emotional control as well. One of her proudest moments, often recounted as a parable of triumph under debilitating circumstances, was when my father flung a drink at her in a chic restaurant. "I didn't move a muscle," she would tell me. "I just sat there throughout the entire meal with my nice dress sopping wet. No one ever guessed there was anything wrong." I listened, and listened well: no one must be allowed to spy the love and sorrow which the heart, in its weakness, fell prey to.

In my senior year of college, I met Danny. A group of us who fancied ourselves acutely liberal, troubled, and artistic often met for lunch in our Missouri college town at a dim café called the Heidelberg. On the day before Valentine's Day 1970, we were speculating on the verdict of the Chicago Seven trial when a new waiter came to the high-backed wooden booth to take our order, and I, with absolutely no hesitation whatsoever, wanted him. Not physically, not yet, but passionately nonetheless. A moment before I had been looking straight ahead, engaged in rational conversation. Then, I was looking up and knowing with a certainty for which nothing had prepared me that he and I must share a love such as Medieval troubadours sang to the accompaniment of lutes: ornate, mythical, tempestuous, doomed.

I have tried to state it less rhapsodically, but that is what I felt the first time I saw Danny. I pause here, sensing that I ought to describe what he looked like, so you'll understand why. Yet I balk. Not because I am inadequate to the task, but because, with that first impression, I saw him whole. When I try to elicit the small details, I lose that first smack of sensation when I was suddenly appalled by the presence of others in this utterly private moment. Considering his lips, his feet, the shadow of beard on his cheeks, memory skips to future moments, as particular features came in to their own.

I could say now that his dark hair fell in unruly waves about his ears and over the back of his neck, that his mind had been on something else that morning when he chose his shirt and slacks. That he was beautiful to look at, and that there was in his eyes a spark of anticipation, as if he'd been informed that something delightful would soon be happening. All this hardly matters. You will picture him in your own way when you recall such an epiphany in your life. We have all had one; maybe one is all we get.

He returned with our order, and now, having emptied the huge metal tray onto the table, he let it hang at his side while he leaned into conversation with one of my friends, an art history professor at the university. Danny, a student in the class, spoke excitedly about a certain 17th century Dutch painting they'd studied, and announced that he'd written a poem about it.

Aha.

"I'm a poet, too," I said. He acknowledged that, but only politely, and I could tell he didn't take me entirely seriously. I approved his caution: only someone who honored poetry as the loftiest expression of the psyche would regard warily another's claim to be its practitioner. Here was further evidence that we had to be together.

But how does a nice girl of 21, scarcely a year past her inauguration into the ultimate mystery between the sexes, let a man know she wants to be with him? I didn't. I couldn't. My way of getting close was circuitous. There was a method to it, but the method was like the angle Emily Dickinson preferred for telling truth: it was slant.

I took to studying at the Heidelberg. He was busy (the big metal tray, his many friends, the way he rounded the door from the kitchen, as if he had all the time in the world), and so was I (I was reading, I was looking something up, I was working on a poem). No less shy about exposing love than I'd been as a teen, I had learned, in intervening years, the art of squirreling away timidity inside bravado. I let him know that despite my frantic scholarship I was pleased to see him. He, in turn, would take a moment to stand before me, one hip cocked to the side, and visit. Once he brought me a beer on the house. There was the day, after the lunch customers had gone back to class, when he plunked himself down on the bench across from me and we began to talk.

Our conversations were literary. We could move with a strut and a confident swing of the arms through hundreds of years of great writing, and this made us feel like pioneers and also like seasoned travelers. These journeys, because of his job, were brief; they were also brilliantly wrought. We were showing off for each other, trying to make the other believe that we had no personal history that mattered as much as the chronicle of what we'd read. For both of us, literature was not an academic study, but an activity that required passion. We spoke animatedly, we spilled over. Often, as we leaned forward on our elbows, our heads nearly touching across the table, exploring some image in Yeats, some turn of scene in Virginia Woolf, it occurred to me how easy it would have been to allow that passion to slip into something more personal. But I was a nice girl. I never let it happen.

This literary foreplay lasted about a month. On a Friday in March I went with a friend to see Luigi Visconti's *The Damned*, which I planned to review for the college newspaper. It was an ugly, soporific, hothouse flower of a movie, and when the lights came on, we shuffled our way dreamily to the exit. Then I saw Danny come down the opposite aisle. In the lobby, my friend concurred with my sudden conviction that such a difficult movie needed at least two viewings to be properly grasped.

I want to rewrite it now. I want to tell you that after she left, I marched straight down that aisle and into his life. I was tired of waiting: that's what I want to say. I'd had enough of bowing with him before other people's genius. Now I was going to grab him out of literature and pull him into my life.

No, what I did was go up to the balcony and scan each dark row until I spotted him. Even then, as if my intent were not already adequately masked, the seat I chose for the site of his discovery of me was not beside, but in front and slightly to the left of him. Already I had squeezed myself so small to avoid bumping the sides of immodesty that I could hardly move.

What did I have to lose? Not virtue, at least in the sense of sexual chastity, not any longer. Pride? A good man's respect? Self-control? My mother would have said so. The example she set, of refusing to want or be wanted by men and of greeting pain as an opportunity to suffer gracefully, had implanted in me the conviction that a woman was safe only when she was as self-contained as a black hole that swallows all light, including its own. I also believed that admitting you wanted something was tantamount to lighting the fuse of its undoing.

He found me, of course, and stage-whispered out to me, and I acted surprised and pleased, and moved back to sit beside him.

So it began, and in the beginning we were exquisite. In the first swell of romance, everything confirms the rightness of this particular pairing — memories of the shallowness of lovers past, the way the new beloved moves through space in evening as he makes his way to you, passages in great literature, the appreciative nods of our friends when they saw us together. Even the clouds metamorphose in celebration of the new union. During the next six risings and settings of the sun, Danny and I saw each other every day. We audited each other's classes, shared our poems (secretly, I thought mine were better; he probably felt the same about his) and, like children with a new best friend, walked around hand and hand in search of people to whom we might introduce this new partner, this spectacular accomplishment. A week after the movie we made love for the first time.

I say that I no longer had my virtue to uphold, but that doesn't mean I'd become a lover. In my junior year, I had engineered the loss of my virginity to a creative writing professor, a man who turned out to be so timid of passion that he never kissed but with his lips avuncularly closed. Because sex with him was so pristine, it did not challenge (or so I persuaded myself) my mother's tenets. It was just one more thing I needed to learn so I could write poems about it.

My second lover was a man who had recently been engaged. He was on the rebound from commitment. He thought me fiery, and liked comparing my drive to his fiancée's preoccupation with copper pots and place settings. But as soon as we lay down on his bed, I was undone. The ampage of his male wanting stunned me. There was nothing polite about it , not a trace of misty rivers and willow boughs. Fear and humiliation made me as unresponsive to him as a subterranean pool to the sun. A few days later I saw him gallantly opening the door of his sports car for his former betrothed.

And so, when I made love to Danny, I brought a passion heavy-laden. He was not like that. He wore life, as the Sufis say, like a loose garment. He had applied to his small hometown draft board for conscientious objector status, because he was opposed to the war in Vietnam and also because he could not accept the right of any person or institution to regulate his life. After graduation he planned to find some callous-building, Hemingwayesque employment through which he could gain experience of the sweatier side of life. The following year he would return to mental labors in a graduate writing program. He liked being taught. One night I watched him try for hours, under a friend's tutelage, to find accord with a harmonica. And he loved pursuing another author's train of thought, delving in to a poem or a passage in a novel and reading it over and over until the words were redolent, like grapes crushed beneath barefeet in a vineyard.

He trusted the time it took to arrive where he was going. And he trusted his mind, unabetted. Although he often drank heavily, he never took drugs in those days when marijuana and psychedelics were accepted aids to enlightenment. Nothing must be allowed to smudge those moments of apotheosis when, in reading or in writing, the mind seizes upon the perfection of some image or intent and sees the whole world reflected there.

He made love carelessly and with delight.

One night in the dark, while I lay grieving over my inadequacy, he told me he loved me. I can hear his voice even now. It was the voice Isaiah might have used if he had been present when the hills at last began to shout and the trees to clap their hands — awed, humble, and a little bit proud of the miracle he'd managed to oversee. "I love you, too," I said. The words were luminous in my throat. But when I spoke them, holding back for dear life, it was with the precision of a carpenter fitting a dovetail joint on a cabinet door.

Danny lived on Pacquin Street, in what must once have been a solid, respectable, clapboard house on a tree-lined block. Under years of occupation by university students, it had relaxed into a middle-aged sag. I remember it as a dark and creaky labyrinth. No one ever bothered to replace the light bulbs in the halls, and tenants had to fumble to unlock the flimsy padlocks that held battered doors close to their jambs. Through the walls and ceilings you could hear people walking and playing music and making love. Danny had never been inspired to decorate. His room was functional, a place to read, write, and sleep, and the sprawl of these these activities was so wide that it formed a sort of decorative signature of its own. The sheets sloughed off the single bed onto the floor . Books toppled over an insubstantial bookcase. The desk was a tumble of papers. Winston cigarette butts overflowed the glass ashtray, which also had to accommodate cones of the Indian incense he liked to burn. In that room we would read poetry aloud to each other, and these were our purest moments. One night in particular remains with me, pivotal, dank with the sorrow of accumulated years. Danny sat in the scruffy easy chair, his bare feet propped on the bed, where I sat facing him. He was reading aloud a translation of Baudelaire:

> Be drunk always. Nothing else matters, this is our sole
> concern. To ease the pain as Time's dread burden weighs

down upon your shoulders and crushes you to earth, you
must be drunk without respite.

Drunk with what? With wine, with poetry, or with virtue,
as you please. But be drunk.

When he finished, he turned the book face down on his lap and
looked to me for confirmation. I saw what he meant: here was the union
between the expression of the ideal and the ideal of expression. This
poem made the link between how we longed to live and, equally if not
more important, how we longed to write about living. Nothing was as
important as abandoning oneself to passion, and the sources of passion
were abundant — in diligent study, hard labor, love, and good, virtuous
causes, such as protesting the war in Vietnam. In the reading and writing
of poetry. Danny sighed, leaned his head against the back of the chair,
and closed his eyes for a moment to savor what he'd read. Then he read
it aloud again.

But for me, watching his rapture, the link between art and life,
between what was ideal and what actual — that link was incomplete.
What would have made it real was reaching out and touching him.
Insouciance was the armament I moved and loved inside. My defense
had toughened over many years, and no impetus from outside of me,
however brute or compassionate, had the power to crack it. But one small
gesture, launched from within, might have brought forth a
transformation. If I could have put my hand out, I would have touched,
before touching him, my own scruples. It would not have felt like armor,
either, but like a bubble, and in the act of reaching, I would have burst it.

Now, many years later, I allow it. It's so simple. I merely lay my palm
on his bare instep. He glances up, smiles. This is no interruption, but an
affirmation of the poetry. I love these feet. All day they are hidden,
holding him up, along with his books, his decisions, his heavy serving
tray. They are the foundation of him, and now they are revealed before
me. As I touch them, I, too, become bared.

But that is not the way it happened. Danny handed the book to me.

I flipped some pages, chose Rimbaud.

My determination to stifle passion grew in proportion to my instinct to express it. You could say I was drunk with virtue. But this was not the ideological intoxication of the political rebel or the ecstatic spiritual inebriation of the mystic. Mine was the dismal, lonely drunkenness of the alcoholic. *Drunk with virtue*: it seems at first an oxymoron, the adjective unsteady, reeking of overindulgence, the noun prim and correct. It described me perfectly. Of shyness, shame, and fear of letting go I had drunk desperately and in isolation. It had gone to my head. And as Friar Laurance, in Romeo and Juliet, observes, "Virtue itself turns to vice, being misapplied."

In the spring of 1970, the clothes, the music, the art and politics were festooned in love and the drive toward liberation, but I could not let go. I held back and held back, until finally I felt that even the warm spring weather was a force that, while it softened and invigorated everyone else, only paralyzed me. Blossoms on trees grieved me. My poems were of lost innocence: the silver moon of myth plundered by science, the grief of Vietnam widows. With Danny I could think of nothing to say because I was incapable of saying the truth: that I loved him, desired him, and wanted him to want me back. Desperately I longed for him to intuit what was wrong and make it well. He couldn't, of course. Such responsibility would be too much for anyone to bear; certainly a 21-year-old college student facing conscription into a foreign war could not handle it. He reacted first with concern, then annoyance, then discontent. By the time of the Kent State murders, I had not heard from him for days. Out of respect, I avoided the places where he could be found.

After graduation, I stayed on in that Missouri college town, sharing an apartment with a friend and doing research for one of my former professors. With nights of beer, marijuana, and guitar music on front porches and luxurious days in an air conditioned office earning money for studying, I was heady with adult independence. I healed. Someone told me Danny was in Illinois, hefting cargo on the docks of the

Mississippi. Two days before I was to leave to drive back east with a friend, I saw him again.

He was driving a motorcycle down a street burning white in the glare of noon when he recognized the back of my hair and made a U-turn. We went for a beer. He too had healed. Having met with benign perplexity from the members of his local draft board, he'd been granted CO status and would never again have to worry about killing and being killed in Vietnam. With his summer earnings he'd bought the forest green 650 Triumph that leaned cockily in the bar's small parking lot, attracting sun. Both of us were wise with experience. We held hands across the table and decided to go to St. Louis.

Maybe it was the joy of holding him for 125 miles, while the sun set at our backs. Maybe emotions crystalize when the air is smacking you in the face, and silos and cars are rushing by like events you choose not to stop for. Maybe the periodic stops we made, to eat and drink beer, to visit his father on the farm, lent a sanctity to this journey, for pilgrims of many faiths and lands know that when the heart is on its path, every crossroad glows with holy import. The wind was wild at our faces and hair, for although Danny had two helmets strapped to the bike, we disdained them, as if, like "Time's dread burden," they would weigh down our shoulders and crush us to earth. I had never ridden on a motorcycle before, but I assure you, I excelled at it.

We were one powerhouse of moving light threading among neon and streetlamps and the dim lights of bars as we toured the city. Toward midnight he called a couple of his friends, who said they'd be glad to put us up for the night. Not knowing how it was between us, they brought pillows and blankets into the living room, and showed us how we could make one bed on the couch and another on the floor. Danny politely offered me the couch and I replied, I know not how: "But I want to sleep with you." It was the first time in my life I had ever admitted to a man how much I liked him.

It was also the first time I had confessed to the unladylike predicament of wanting. I had little time to waver. There was a hasty smoothing of bedding on the rug, and then I experienced for the first time the sensational inadequacy of my mother's adjective, "beautiful," for that exuberant ride through joy that is physical love. Colors bloomed behind my eyes. Forms rounded and burst in the way we moved. He was delicious. I lost myself and found myself as I found and was found by him, and together we swam through a marvelous awakening.

I want to make this the end of the story. Compositionally, it's a good place to stop. I can tell you that from here on out I relished sex and shed my strictures against speaking of love, and that, to a great extent, will be true. In this version, sadly, Danny's way and mine diverge, although we continue, perhaps all our lives, to be on the lookout for each other, especially in bars and at poetry readings. That is not the way it was.

The following spring I met a man with I whom I contrived to hitchhike across the United States to California. We travelled light, but we were conscious of leaving much behind, including the shackles of possessions and the uninspired demands of adulthood. Once we were on the road, however, our yearning to move freely, now sated, dissolved into pickiness. The countryside was splendid, but there was little we could find to like in each other. By the time we reached my old college town, I'd plotted an escape. I called Danny's father, who called his son, still working on the docks. Moments later, he called me back, and we agreed to meet at a friend's house on the outskirts of town.

In the middle of the night I awoke to his arrival. He had traveled more than 200 miles to get to me and made the trip in less than three hours. He roared through that sleepy aluminum-sided block of houses, with its plastic wading pools and spindly trees, and only slowed the motorcycle when he'd spun it onto the scant front lawn. I stood naked in the dark window of a small bedroom furnished only with a twin bed mattress, and I watched him, not seeing me as he threw his leg over the motorcycle and turned on his heel toward the door. Never had I suffered such ardor.

We spent the next day and a half together, all of it in that nondescript house, most of it in the uncurtained bedroom, where revolutions of sunlight and dark lent a cosmic significance to our union.

Danny, too, was headed for California. In a couple of weeks he'd be leaving his job to spend the summer touring the country, and in September he would enter the graduate writing program at Syracuse University. I was bold enough to suggest we make the trip together, but he wanted to have his adventure solo, and though I was disappointed, I understood. I was glad I'd asked.

So we parted. My traveling companion and I came to an understanding, which lasted, with partial success, for about two-thirds of the Lower Forty-Eight. Two months later, just after I'd gotten back to Connecticut and was trying to patch together the adulthood I'd tried to forfeit, I got a letter from Danny. He was in Mill Valley, just outside San Francisco, and he had started a literary magazine. "Send poems!!" he charged.

A week later my fat envelope came back unopened. A ballpoint message scrawled next to the address stated, with controlled succinctness: "Deceased."

I called his father, who told me Danny had been killed six days earlier in a motorcycle accident. I was not surprised to learn that he had not been wearing a helmet. And when I thought of the speed with which he had torn through the miles to reach me that night, I thought I knew something about the way he must have been traveling, and I imagined that, just before the crash, he had been reveling in motion, wind, and all the poems he was gathering around him.

Well into the winter I was writing poems telling him how much I had loved him.

TRAVEL IN A DANGEROUS COUNTRY

Two barred owls peer down from an astroturf-covered perch as Wendy Thomlinson, an intern at the Raptor Center in Woodstock, Vermont, enters the cage and latches the door behind her. The owls' plumage is buff, cinnamon, soot, white, and gray, the colors of winter woods. They move no muscle except their eyes. Their expression is both wary and flirtatious, the latter impression conveyed by the nictating membrane, an inner eyelid that protects the birds from twigs and long grasses as they glide low toward prey and that winks over their pupil every few seconds. The wariness is that of two old friends who suspect that afternoon tea is about to be interrupted by some nuisance involving a maintenance crew.

Wendy swings in the direction of the owls with a net and, their suspicions confirmed, they rise lazily from the perch and head instinctively for the end of the cage, where I wait outside. Finding it impassable, they turn and fly in the opposite direction, toward a doorway just below the ceiling that offers passage into a second cage. A moment later, two more owls zoom in, talons extended, from a third cage, where they have been urged up by another net-bearing intern. They hit the vinyl-coated mesh above me with their feet and spin back again, like swimmers flipping themselves around at the end of the pool so as not to break their momentum.

Like all the birds at the Raptor Center, a division of the non-profit environmental education and research organization, The Vermont Institute of Natural Science (VINS), these owls were brought here because they were sick or injured. Now they have recuperated and are almost well enough to be released back to the wild. First, however, each bird has to pass two crucial tests: it must be able to fly and it must be able to catch prey. The flight cage, actually three adjoining cages each thirty feet long, was built to satisfy the first requirement. Flying laps and negotiating the openings, which are set at angles to prevent it from taking the easy way out and simply flying in a straight line, the owl strengthens the wing muscles that have weakened during its captivity. When its flight is strong and easy, the bird proceeds to the second and final test. The recovery diet, a frozen mouse or rat injected with a little warm water and served in the food box in its cage, will be replaced by a live creature that the interns will turn loose under a covering of hay and twigs made a little denser and more challenging each day. Only after the staff is satisfied that the bird can, in the words of a local veterinarian, "one hundred percent earn its living in the wild," will they release it.

The flight cage is the transitional corridor the birds must pass through to return to health. It is the avian treadmill on which they exercise to regain mobility and self-sufficiency in their natural domain. What do the owls experience, I wonder, as they do their laps? Owls have very acute hearing. When an owl's ears pick up a sound — a vole, say, gnawing seeds under leaves — specialized neurons in the brain translate it to a precise three-dimensional map of the space the bird must maneuver to reach its prey. What happens to this sense when the owl is confined to a cage? Does it atrophy like the wing muscles, and is it then gradually reinvigorated with each lap, so the bird is mentally geared up, as well as physically fit, to return to the wild? Or does the bird, confined to its perch, tune in to all kinds of sounds emanating from the woods, the Raptor Center infirmary, and the barn downhill, where VINS holds its programs? And does this sophisticated activity of its physiology ache for completion in a foot-full of prey?

Physician and author Richard Selzer calls surgery "travel in a dangerous country." Indeed, any venture into the life-and-death processes of another is risky, no matter how skilled the healer. How can anyone truly know the contours of another's illness, or discern tracks, so faint as to be almost undetectable, that could lead to recovery? The difficulty is compounded when the treatment is being conducted by members of one species on behalf of another.

"We try to understand not just the physical, but the psychological needs of the birds," Raptor Center director Julie Tracy tells me. "We try to think like the birds. Barred owls are generally pretty mellow and easy to handle. An accipiter, like a goshawk, is a very high-strung bird. They move around a lot, they're very fast flyers in the woods. If you have an accipiter as a patient, and the bird is holding still and letting you handle it without causing any problems, you know you have a very sick bird. We raise hamsters for prey-testing snowy owls, because hamsters behave like lemmings, which these birds eat in the wild. They turn around and try to bite their predators when they're caught. So you've got to really know what the bird needs. What does the bird need for security and shelter? What is its behavior like? Does the bird normally stand on one leg all day long or is there a problem? That's the kind of diagnostic work we do."

Like Julie, the rest of the staff — Raptor Rehabilitation Coordinator Charity Uman and four interns, all in their early twenties — tend to be pragmatic about what they do. But their diagnostic techniques are regularly supplemented by another, less teachable skill. Charity first dismisses it as "common sense" and gives what she considers an obvious example. When she is under stress, she makes it a habit to pause and do deep-breathing exercises before she approaches a bird. "A cat or a dog will snuggle up to you and comfort you if you've had a bad day," she says. "But a bird of prey will sense your tension and pick up on it."

Common sense, maybe, to those who work with wild animals, but this sensibility takes time to develop. Charity describes the time she was struggling to treat a goshawk who happened to be a particularly nervous member of this skittish species. Julie came by, observed for a moment, and then, quite spontaneously, began to tweak at the bird's feathers with her fingers, as if she were another bird grooming it with a beak. The bird calmed down immediately. "It was amazing," Charity says. "This bird was so paranoid you couldn't get close to it, and it was letting Julie touch it! She just has this ability to tune in to what a bird needs."

There was no precedent for what Julie did, no textbook recommendation of feather-preening as an antidote to goshawk anxiety.

Julie simply followed her intuition and stepped over the boundary that normally separates humans from animals, and, because there was something calm and confident and apparently non-invasive about what she was doing, the goshawk consented to move beyond its own customary boundaries. The two met in a metaphysical fringe territory, where an exchange of energies took place — one voluntarily given, the other welcomed.

"What do you want?" I ask a peregrine falcon the next morning.

The bird perches on a bough covered with astroturf in a large cage that looks out over a ripple of high hills and a broad, overcast sky. Although a couple of perches in the cage are dry and protected, she has chosen to stand in an open area, where misty rain falls onto her body. With her helmet of black feathers and her protruding brow, she looks like a warrior in contemplation.

Her wing web was damaged when she alit on a downed power line; her condition worsened when the people who found her, excited by the notion of possessing a wild creature as a pet, kept her in an old dog kennel for several weeks. There she developed bumblefoot, an infection caused when a normally active bird must stand idly on a perch that is too big or too small, causing her weight to be unevenly distributed. The bumblefoot has nearly healed in the year she has been at the Raptor Center, but she can fly no more than eight or ten feet. When she is better, the staff will train her to become a "teaching bird," calm enough to stand on a perch before wide-eyed children while a VINS lecturer describes her habits in the wild.

Once this bird was one of the fastest flyers in the world, able to dive toward her prey at speeds of up to 200 miles per hour. Her eyesight, eight times more acute than that of humans, enabled her to spot prey two miles off, and she could snatch a songbird in mid-flight. Biologists, not known for creative flair in the naming of wild things, have been inspired to call the moves the peregrine executes in flight "sky dancing," "parachuting," and "whirling." The poet Robinson Jeffers envisioned the peregrine falcon as an emblem of "fierce consciousness."

"What do you want?" I ask the peregrine. For I cannot believe that such a skilled being, a long distance traveler and aerial acrobat, is not fully cognizant of her condition. I get no response, although I am aware of her awareness of me. Wildness radiates from her. She may be in captivity, but she has not submitted to a thing. Erect, focused, alert, she seems to have consented, for now, to wait for what may happen next. I get these impressions not through words, but through her presence, which reveals itself gradually as I stand in the rain outside her cage. Still, I long for something more. I long to brush consciousness with her in that fringe territory that belongs neither to her nor to me, but that is accessible to both of us if we are willing to go there.

Most birds who come to the Raptor Center have been the victims, deliberately or inadvertently, of humans. They have been shot by guns and hit by cars. They have flown into picture windows and been attacked by pet cats. They have lost their nests to chain saws and their habitats to bulldozers. (The interns wave nets at the birds in the flight cage not only to impel them to fly but also to remind them that humans tend not to have their best interests at heart.)

Once, according to the myths and legends of many people, the ways of animals and humans were less disjunct, and both species regularly crossed the line between them. Then the healing process worked both ways. Humans could heal animals and animals could heal people. Many Native American legends tell of a person or even an entire community that was rescued from danger by an animal. Often, all the animal asked in return was protection for itself and its kind. In a Lakota story, White Buffalo Calf Woman appears to the people who have prepared a sacred medicine lodge according to her instructions and teaches them the lore of the Buffalo people, including the correct way to hunt and how to carve and smoke the sacred pipe. She promises that, as long as the Lakota people honor the Buffalo people, the animal will provide for them, giving them its meat as food, its fur as robes and the covering of lodges, its bones and sinew as tools. Thus, the well-being of both species is safeguarded, with each devoted to the long life of the other.

Shamans from Siberia to Peru have relied on animals to assist them in their work as intercessors between those who ail and the otherworldly beings that have caused the ailment. To the shaman, the whole cosmos is alive. All animals, waters, plants, rocks, diseases and states of mind are not only cognizant, but able to communicate with all other forms of life. The more powerful the shaman, the more skillfully she can mediate among them. But she never ventures forth alone, for, like the modern surgeon, she knows that the country of sickness is perilous. She travels in the company of spirit guides, the animals who come to meet her when she enters a trance state. They counsel her how to negotiate obstacles, what herbs to gather for medicine, how to find the sickness and coax or rout it out. Sometimes the guide enables the shaman to assume its own animal form, so she can experience fleetness, a keen sense of smell, stealth, or sureness of aim that she could never attain merely by trying to pattern her own behavior that way. Diving deep into the realm where all living creatures are peers and paddling with the feet of her animal teacher, the shaman experiences the commonality and the complexity of all creatures, and uses this knowledge on behalf of her patients.

A Navajo friend of mine says that when an animal comes into your life, it means to teach you something. It brings you medicine. "Medicine" is the name many Native Americans use for a vision or counsel bestowed on them by an animal. The gift holds a special power, for it represents the animal's recognition and encouragement of a person's own most valuable attributes, now enhanced by the attributes of the animal. A bonding occurs that lasts a lifetime. This power must never be wielded over others, for it is sacred. The recipient uses it for the benefit of her community, always acknowledging that it came to her by the grace of the animal.

I thought about the mysterious power of animals and medicine on the occasion when I first heard about the Raptor Center. My brother, who lives about seventy miles north of Woodstock, was driving home one day when he saw a barred owl standing in the road. He stopped beside it, but it didn't move, so he wrapped it up in his jacket and took it to the Raptor Center. The staff examined the bird and found it had a fractured wing. They told Frederick they expected the bird to recover fully and invited him to be present for its release.

When my brother told me this story, I began to nurse the wild hope that the owl had deliberately placed itself in his path. For years, Frederick has suffered from debilitating bouts of depression. He has been a patient in many hospitals, tried a pharmacopoeia of medications, consulted numerous psychologists. Nothing works for long. Nobody can figure out what's wrong. But when an animal comes into your life, it means to teach you something. Maybe, I thought, the physical act of saving the owl's life, combined with the mental energy he was now devoting to its recovery, would produce a tonic potent enough to cure him of his own illness. I didn't know about the flight cage at the time, but I did imagine that as the owl thrived and regained its ability to fly, my brother might regain the use of his emotional wings.

Things did not work out the way I'd hoped. Frederick was unable to attend the triumphant occasion of the owl's release, because he was back in the hospital. And although the memory of its weeks in captivity is now presumably only a faint smudge on the owl's awareness, my brother becomes more and more a captive of his illness. He has not earned his own living in years. During the weeks of halcyon relief, he tries valiantly to patch together a life for himself, but he is forgetting how to exist in days made up of ordinary chores, unpredictable frustrations, little riffs of joy.

The Navajos say that illness is caused by imbalance. In a healthy, natural state, the Earth and all that exists upon it are composed of complementary pairs: for example, male/female, light/dark, dryness/moisture. When one of the pair overpowers the other, sickness results. By sickness they mean not just physical aches and pains, but personal misfortune and social ills as well. When I look at my brother's life, I see a world out of balance. What is frightening and unruly has subsumed the ordinary; nothing can be relied on. The raptors are the victims of imbalance of the opposite kind. Their habitats are under siege from all kinds of environmental "taming" seen as necessary to human comfort and convenience, and people have little idea how to behave in, and with, the wilderness that's left. If an animal did come forth to tell us what it needed or to advise us how we might use our truest aptitudes, who among us would be able to listen?

Yet many people yearn for that connection between themselves and animals, even those who pride themselves on studying nature objectively, assiduously avoiding projections of nature's ways that smack of anthropomorphizing. Even Henry David Thoreau, a passionate naturalist with a certain disdain for excessive anthropomorphizing, exulted when a sparrow alit on his shoulder: "I felt that I was more distinguished by that circumstance than I should have been by any epaulet I could have worn."

In conversations with Raptor Center staff and volunteers I notice that a genuine respect for the birds' innate nature is often mixed with an unstated hope that the feeling might be reciprocated. These young men and women frequently veer away from the subject of birds who are recuperating and will be released to focus instead on their progress with the teaching birds. "I can't believe how calm Aquila was with me today," Heather Hersh, a young volunteer, exclaims about a one-winged red-tail hawk she's training. Even Raptor Center founder Sally Laughlin, when I ask for some memorable stories about her years in Woodstock, first recalls a great-horned owl that was released only to return to her home the following winter to tap on her window with its beak, begging for food.

What made such moments memorable was not that the birds had become tame, for they had not, but that bird and human were able, briefly but fully, to perceive the otherness of the one in its company and to recognize that something could be shared precisely because of that otherness. "The birds know I don't want anything from them except to admire their beauty and wildness," Heather tells me by way of explaining the uncanny tendency most birds have to relax with her. As I myself experienced in the peregrine falcon's presence, the qualities of beauty and wildness can radiate like light from a bird. To witness, perhaps even to absorb a bit of it, feels like a blessing. It seems possible that for these intuitive, highly sensitive birds of prey, appreciation unattached to fear, impatience, or the greed to possess is a gift as well.

According to evolutionary biologist E.O. Wilson, much of the human species currently suffers from "biophobia," the fear of nature. The opposite of this sickness is biophilia, which Wilson defines as "the innate tendency to focus on life and lifelike processes," and which may actually be of genetic rather than psychological origin. His "biophilia hypothesis" proposes that *homo sapiens* may have benefited in several ways from a deep emotional need to be close to nature. Just as the wings of the owls in the Raptor Center atrophy when they aren't used, so, too, could this behavioral trait weaken with prolonged immersion in urban life, and people would find themselves, first, indifferent to, later even hostile to nature. However, the trend may not be irreversible. As the owls regain the power of their wing muscles through exercise, we might be able to revitalize this critical part of our makeup just by renewing our contact with nature.

But where are the flight cages we can enter to work our way back to the natural world? What step can we take to share the fierce consciousness of a peregrine falcon?

We might begin by observing a few simple rules of interspecies etiquette. Humility is the most important quality. In an encounter with a wild creature, humans aren't in charge, a status that may take some getting used to. And so we cultivate a second ethic: unconditional patience. We don't rush toward the animal, smiling and effusive, eager to take control and leave a strong first impression — manners, we have been taught, that assure success in business and society. We wait. We let the animal make the first move. As Julie Tracy remarked when describing the qualities she looks for in interns, "People who don't have a natural respect for someone else's personal space tend not to do well with birds." In the fringe territory, we must suspend disbelief. Familiar patterns of cause and effect often have little meaning, whereas intuition and flares of insight or emotion can be as genuine as they are inexplicable.

A woman who participated in a psycho-spiritual wilderness trip I led in the Utah Canyonlands was a social worker. Her husband of twenty years had recently died, and she had just committed her mother, suffering from Alzheimer's, to a nursing home. She had not spent much time outside the large city where she had always lived, and she was nervous about the wildlife she might encounter. Sitting by herself on a high, sunny mesa, however, this woman found herself telling her entire life story to a lizard, which sat perfectly still in front of her until she had finished. In all her relationships, she had assumed the role of caretaker and was unable to ask for comfort and counsel for herself. What she learned from the lizard was that nature is generous enough to bear witness to her sorrow and compassionate enough to weave it lightly into the fabric that is all life on Earth.

Moreover, it is not just personal insight that can be garnered from a brief and startling encounter with a wild creature, but, as in the Lakota story of White Buffalo Woman, a wholly new paradigm for both species. American conservationist Bert Schwarzschild had traveled to Italy for the express purpose of hiking on Mount Subasio, where St. Francis preached his famous sermon to the birds. As he walked, he grew increasingly distressed by the silence in the air and the litter of shotgun shells on the ground, for songbirds in Italy are shot as game. That night, as he lay in his sleeping bag, a nightingale began to sing in a bush very close to him, and in a moment of absolute clarity, Schwarzschild heard the bird asking directly for his help. When he got back to the United States, he launched an international campaign that resulted in the designation of Mount Subasio as a wildlife refuge. Simply by paying attention and suspending disbelief long enough to get the message his heart needed, he was able to benefit humans and animals alike.

Driving north from Woodstock to visit my brother before heading back home, I think about a conversation I had with Charity this morning. As we walked past the cages where the birds perched, silent and watchful, and possessed, ultimately, of a consciousness utterly mysterious to us humans, she described the way birds who have fully recovered are released. "By that time, you've removed the jesses, the leather straps we keep on their legs while they're here. What happens a lot of times is that the bird doesn't know yet that it's free, so it just stands there in your hands. You lower your hands a little bit, just a couple of inches, and the bird feels the gravity and pulls against it and that's when it realizes it can fly. And off it goes." So, in the end, it is the bird's natural proclivity to be airborne that sets it free. And the last act of assistance offered by the hand of the rehabilitator is simply to serve as a launching platform.

Of course, not every bird can be released. Those whose injuries would be severely crippling must be euthanized. Others, for example those who have lost the use of a wing or sight in one eye, often stay on to become teaching birds and, when necessary, surrogate parents to orphaned babies of their species. Sometimes, then, there's no way to get back to the wild, for even the fairly straightforward passages of the flight cage remain unnegotiable. In this case, the bird will come to terms with life in captivity or, failing that, simply give up and die, an acquiescence to fate known to every creature who has lived by the guidelines of predator-and-prey.

What, I wonder, as I speed along the highway, will become of the wild and beautiful peregrine? Then I think: maybe the same ultimatum is presented to humans as well. Maybe, after long periods of sickness, we too must choose between returning to our natural habitat and remaining in unnatural captivity. If so, what will become of my brother? What will become of us humans if we forget what is required to receive the medicine of animals?

Maybe we, like the birds, aren't bound by the jesses we assume hold us back. Maybe simple attentiveness to the natural world that surrounds us is our own best launch back to a deeper relationship with it. Open to the possibilities of a meeting with a wild creature, wanting nothing but to admire, we too could fly across old boundaries to a fringe territory where both we and the animals could experience the country of health.

11 INTERVENTIONS FROM AUGUST IN THE 10 DAYS OF YOUR DYING

1. **Wildflowers.** Such color, such petal-work on the trail behind our village: Queen Anne's lace, daisies, goldenrod, wild pea, purple vetch, thistle, meadowsweet — I gather them, remembrance of splendor to bring home to you.

2. **Oak tree roots.** Heading to the park across from the hospital to call friends with the news, I find no seat but this nexus of roots, rough and exposed as nerves.

3. **A breath of rose.** Right there on a patch of lawn between entrance and sidewalk, a bush of magenta blooms goes ignored by so many worried people. I cross over, inhale a dose of resolve.

4. **Carrots.** I text you a photo of my handful, fresh from the garden, incomparably orange, soil clinging to the roots and grooves. Remember when I planted those seeds in their pale, thin sheaths, while you directed from your chair?

5. **Rain.** After they reveal your prognosis, after we hold each other, bear each other down into the unthinkable, after you call your three grown children, a thunderstorm breaks and even the window weeps.

6. **White sun offered on a golden saucer of cloud.** On a walk before I leave for the hospital, I watch it rising over the mill pond, as if the unprecedented was ordinary.

7. **An emerging peach.** Fuzzy and firm, the color of river stone, the only fruit on the tree we planted on our anniversary. If it grows to

ripen, I promise you, I will savor it.

8.   **A window of woods, a window of garden.** Even in the matter of picking a hospice room, we choose our most likely redeemers.

9.   **The taste of basil and garlic.** Every garden you've ever tended flavors this pesto I made last week and eat by your bedside as you sleep.

10.   **A Snickers bar.** Back in the hospital, you asked me to bring one, but it's only now, after eating nothing for days, that you think of it. "We'll share it," you say. Two bites each, back and forth. Our last meal together.

11.   **Katydids.** I have kissed you goodbye, made the calls, packed our things. I step out into a hot summer midnight to the paeans of katydids singing in the trees. The only conceivable response is to set down our bags and bow.

KISSED BY FIRE

s I walked out of the somber rooms of the funeral home into the bright August sunlight, carrying my husband's ashes, I teetered between two realities: *This, now, is him, in his entirety* and *This has absolutely nothing to do with him.*

I had been at Andy's bedside in the hospice a few days earlier, and when he died, I had seen the life force loft right out of him. It was a holy moment. For two and a half days I had sat with him, holding his hand, stroking his cheek, doing ceremony to ease the way to his final transition, talking with him and then, when he lapsed into unconsciousness, only *to* him. In those minutes after he took in his last breath, before I walked down the hall to notify the night nurse, it had been the astonishing beauty and mystery of the passage that had seized me, how dying was nothing like falling asleep, the comforting image adults give to children to explain death. Nor was that instant of departure a mere collection of physical symptoms — a stopped heart, a sudden settling of the limbs. Andy had left, completely left.

Yet now, as I walked across the parking lot, I carried another incarnation of him: his life-free body, translated by fire into something else. After death, there is a bodily aftermath of death, and this was our version of it, my husband's and mine: ash.

After untold years of mourning and searching, the goddess Isis at last finds the remains of her brother/lover Osiris in the realm of Byblos. His body lies in the sarcophagus that his jealous brother Set had tricked him into trying out for size before nailing him into it. The sarcophagus had floated down the river until it encountered an enormous tamarisk tree, which embraced it in its branches. So enchanted was the king of Byblos by this beautiful, fragrant tree that he had it cut down and refashioned as a pillar, still clutching its divine acquisition, to hold up the roof of his palace. There Isis ceases her wandering to hold vigil, mourning and singing by the entwined phenomenon of coffin, tree, and pillar. She braids the hair of the queen's maids and scents them with ambrosia, making them so beautiful that the queen entrusts the mysterious visitor with the care of her infant child. At night, when everyone is asleep, Isis lays the baby in a fire to burn off his mortality, while she takes the form of a swallow, circling round and round the pillar. When the queen comes upon this eerie scene one night, she snatches her child from the fire, robbing him of immortality.

A very similar myth arose in Greece as the story of Demeter stopping in Eleusis as she grieves the loss of her daughter, Persephone, abducted by Hades into the Underworld. She, too, nurses the royal child in fire. Her ceremony of mourning and creation is also interrupted when the king grabs back the child and condemns him to an ordinary human life. The similarity of the stories likely comes from the geographical proximity and trade relations between ancient Egypt and Greece. But it is the psychological, cultural endurance of the myth that continues to matter. In both tales, a mourning goddess partners with fire in an effort to empower life.

The pot that held my husband's ashes was one he had made. He and his friend, the artist Phil Sims, had decided twenty years earlier that they would build wood-fired kilns, one in each of their yards in our small rural community of northeastern Pennsylvania. In preparation they read books, made sketches, studied a variety of kilns, and had endless discussions. The supplies arrived — high-fire bricks, metal for the smokestack, pyrometers to track the rise and fall of the heat. They worked for weeks, building the kilns, constructing sheds around them to keep the operation and the operators dry, cutting wood. Over the years, they had dozens of firings. Andy, Phil and his partner, Kai O'Connor, and occasionally other potters and conscripted friends took turns in long shifts of feeding wood into the kiln and monitoring the temperature. You could glimpse the alchemical process by removing a cube of brick from the spyhole to peer into the inferno of creative action. But once the process was underway, the fire was in charge.

As they worked, Andy and Phil would sit by the kiln in battered lawn chairs, drinking coffee and debating. Should they drive the fire with fast-burning locust wood or let it build more gradually with maple or ash? Should they push the temperature higher or close the kiln now? Potters monitor kiln temperature not just with a pyrometer but with cones, ceramic pyramids that are slightly larger and thinner than cones of incense and positioned in a row on a small base. Composed of ceramic materials, they're designed to start drooping from the tip as the heat builds in the kiln. You can see them through the spyhole as they bend over one at a time until they sag. Phil wanted to aim for Cone 14, or 2,523 degrees Fahrenheit; Andy argued that Cone 13, about 2,455 degrees, was ideal, that higher temperatures burned off the metallic oxide that gave a sheen to the pots. A body in a cremation fire burns at much lower temperatures, around Cone 07, or about 1,800 degrees, the temperature at which you would fire porcelain.

Despite all the disputing and discussions, drawings and evaluations they made, what really fascinated both these artists was the surprises the fire wrought: the way it played over the pots and metamorphosed them into objects of texture, sheen, and color utterly different from the raw shapes that had gone into the kiln. Sometimes the fire caused glaze to drip from a pot on an upper shelf and pool like a liquefied jewel in the pot below, or it painted one side of a pot with scaly ash, while leaving the opposite side with a silky gloss, effects called "kiln gifts." The firing process also produced what are known as "kisses," when two pots leaned together in the kiln, and one pot "kissed" its neighbor, losing a bit of its own glaze, which it deposited on the adjacent pot, like a smack of lipstick. For Andy every pot told a story that you could explore by turning the piece around in your hands. Sometimes, he would deliberately reform one side of a pot, cutting into the wet clay and pressing the pieces unevenly back together with his hands. Or he would paint a simple graphic design around the pot, so that the eyes and hands could journey around it together. He knew that he was only the first artist, that fire would take over where he left off. The fire is the master artist, the final arbiter, the ultimate seducer.

The myths of Isis and Demeter and the fire-giving life they attempt to impart in the midst of their own grieving remain with us after thousands of years. Why is deep, stabbing grief paired with infancy and immortality? These stories tell us that, even at a time of immense sorrow, we have the power, maybe even the obligation, to take up the care of something new and unseasoned and burn life into it. We do not try convince ourselves that our grief will be salved by this creative fire. We know we'll have to keep trudging down the long road of heartbreak, fighting at times even to breathe for one more minute through that terrible loss. And yet, say the myths, we must tend to life, not just after the sorrow wanes, but in the very maelstrom of it.

I didn't sit long that night by the bed that held the body of my husband. I felt almost desperate to go outside, to inhale the night air and find out if, in fact, I was capable of taking my first steps into a world I would now have to walk without him. After calling Andy's children and a few friends, I packed our things and drove from the hospice along dark and sleeping roads to the home of Phil and Kai. For hours we sat around the wood-burning fire pit on their deck, drinking tea and telling stories about Andy. The light from the fire illumined our small circle as coyotes howled in the dark woods behind their house.

In the modern cremation process, the body, lying in a plain wooden container, is pushed into the cremation chamber. For one and a half to two hours, it burns. Hair, eyelashes, the soft flesh of the inner thigh, the hands that curled to countless tasks, the stomach, the heart, the throat that swallowed food, the tongue that expressed love and wonder, anger and ideas — fire caresses and devours it all. Whereas the fire in a kiln embellishes the shape that's given to it, a cremation fire dissolves. When, I got home with the pot holding Andy's ashes and opened it, I sifted through the white powder, looking for any trace of his wedding ring, which I had asked the funeral director to leave on his finger. There was no sign of it. Nothing was left but chalky white ash and tiny gobbets of bone.

To hold the ash that is all that remains of your loved one is a jarring experience. It is a thing of no meaning that you feel ought to be meaningful. *This is Andy. This* was *Andy. This is the living transformed to death.* I said things like that to myself every time I held that pot of ash — and I couldn't grasp my own words. What does fire-wrought ash have to do with a human life? Disrobed of life, then taken by fire, a human had become elemental. Still, it was him, and it seemed right that what was left of him rest in a place that would feel like home. I decided that, instead of putting the pot of ashes in some lofty place, like a mantle or a special altar, I would settle it on the back porch, on the old enamel table that he used to pot seedlings for the garden and where he deposited in an old metal cookie tin the dried flower heads and interesting stones and pieces of wood he found.

Fire creates. Fire cooks. Fire kills. Fire also kisses. It kisses death from life and life from death. It kisses shine out of dullness, powder out of solid, black char out of green, moist growth. Fire is radical, potent, and strange. Potters and glass blowers who partner with it are daredevils willing to risk control for magic. Often they sacrifice not just control but the entirety of their envisioned creation, for fire breaks, blows, burns, busts, and shatters if the artist slips up just for an instant — or even if everything goes as planned. An article in *Parabola*'s 1978 issue on Inner Alchemy quotes Shaikh Ahmad Ahsa, who compares the alchemical process to the making of glass. The process begins when the philosopher-artist fuses silica and potash. If the glass that results is itself fused, it becomes even more brilliant. And if that sparkling crystal is melted once again and the alchemist's mysterious white elixir is projected onto it, "lo and behold! it becomes diamond. It is still glass and yet no — it is something other but not so, it is certainly itself but itself after undergoing all these trials." The contents of the pot on the back porch was Andy himself, but himself after undergoing all the trials of a lifetime.

I, too, turned out to be still myself as I learned how to survive without him. I had always thought that, if Andy died, I would not want to live, but I was wrong. When it seemed that grief was on the verge of extinguishing my own life, I did not hold back. I wailed and wept and hit the bottom, time and time again. And then, oddly but consistently, I would find myself being shoved out of that torturous pit, as if by the grief itself, which, once it gained my surrender, could no longer hold me. I would get up, sit on the front porch and listen to the birds, or harvest the vegetables from Andy's garden, or call a friend. I saw beauty everywhere every day and felt inexpressible gratitude for the love of my friends.

About a month after Andy died, on the night of the dark moon, I did a vigil in our meadow. I lit a small fire and kept it burning as I spoke aloud to Andy about my regrets, my memories, my love. The pot of ashes rested on a stone opposite me, its chalk-colored sides shimmering in the light of a fire that, this time, did not touch it. As a damp gray dawn spread over the sky, I spread some of his ashes over the trees and bushes we had planted together and that he had so carefully tended, and over the plants in his vegetable garden. I poured ash into smaller pots that I gave to Andy's two sons and to Phil, and then I wrapped the pot with the remainder in a piece of beautiful fabric.

A few weeks later I started to look for a new home in a different area. Sometimes I wondered if I was rushing things; some of my friends thought so too. But I sensed that those cautions were like the protective instincts of the royal parents in the myths: worry that such a large, combustible action might burn me even more. To me the grief invoked a call of matching intensity in the direction of survival. To ignore it would be to wither into half-life. I also finished writing my new book in those first few months alone and, with my nonprofit organization, created an online Global Day of Mourning for the losses and gifts of the coronavirus pandemic. Every day I grieved the death of my beloved, and every day I grappled to grab hold of life. As I got settled in my new home in upstate New York, I decided to buy a green burial plot. One day my unembalmed body will be wrapped in a shroud and laid in the ground, mingling with the rest of Andy's ashes, which I interred there. Ash and bone will sift together as fire, soil, water, and air mix us together in the Earth's final, ongoing kiss.

PART IV
Learning To Love The Waste

CARING FOR THE WASTE

(This essay was published in 1989, at a time when I was searching for some way to face hurt places on Earth and reconnect with them.)

In the late 1980s, two decades before the gas drilling arrived in rural northeastern Pennsylvania, where I live, word got out that a farm nearby was under consideration as the site for a low-level nuclear waste dump. My first reaction was, "No way!" But even as I joined other activists to fight the dump, I began fighting another, more personal battle as well: I started preparing to cherish that waste.

The prospect of living around the bend from a mounting repository of radioactive material was so terrifying that any but the most reckless, naïve, or mercenary person cannot even bear to consider it. Even the company that would operate the facility and whose objective at that initial stage was to assure us that all would be well, managed to frighten us with its reassurances. Besides promising that they would pay our school taxes, provide jobs, and give us free medical exams if we let them come, the company informed us that they would train school children in procedures to be followed if something went wrong. A friend vehemently declared, "If they build it here, I'm putting the house up for sale. And if anyone asks why, I won't say, because nobody will come near this area if they know the truth."

But how, I had to ask myself, could I refuse this waste when I have helped create it? My community isn't powered by nuclear energy, and I didn't work in a lab or industry that uses radioactive materials. But if I claimed that all of life is interconnected (and I do), then I had to be prepared to accept that my society's waste is my own as well. Besides, my lifestyle, which I liked to think of as holistic and environmentally astute, was not all that pure. In the summer my husband and I picked fresh vegetables and fruits from our own garden, but in the winter we bought them from health food stores which trucked them east from organic farms in California. Sometimes, when the weather was very hot, I indulged by turning on the car air conditioner. And as a writer, I used paper, which demands the felling of trees. What I used, used energy, and what uses energy makes waste.

According to David Powless, an Oneida engineer who is currently involved in the clean-up of waste generated by this country's first nuclear plant in Hanford, Washington, it is a mistake to hate the waste, which, after all, is a natural byproduct of any organism that feeds itself in order to live. "If we approach the waste with good intention, as if it were an orphan abandoned by the process it served, and if we say to it, 'I have come to work with you to bring you back to the circle of life,' then we will be shown the way," he told me once. "All purification is through the earth. Our purification is when those wastes find a home and become decontaminated."

What, I asked myself as I gathered information about the half-life of heavy metals and the reliability of concrete versus steel storage containers, what must I do to respect such a monstrous presence as nuclear waste? How can ordinary people work with such a burden for the purification of all?

I took inspiration from Avalokiteshvara, the Buddha's principal bodhisattva. He chose to delay nirvana and to remain among civilization until all other sentient beings had attained enlightenment. His sacrifice was not only his own rest and comfort, but also a determination not to shut his eyes on the sorrows of the world and to reach out his hand to help.

I knew that I, too, had to be willing to sacrifice, a word that comes from the Latin roots meaning to make sacred. First, I had to accept waste as a byproduct of my own energetic journey through life and understand that it would not go away, even if some other community, not mine, were to be assigned the burden of hosting the radioactive waste facility.

Also, I had to be conscious of consuming less. Only if my generation could agree to deny ourselves the high standard of living that we regard as intrinsic to our pursuit of happiness could we guarantee some happiness for our children and for all who will have to tend our waste, nuclear and non-nuclear, for at least as many generations into the future as have peopled this land since Columbus first set foot upon it.

Finally, I had to consider the future if my community lost its fight. Writer and deep ecologist Joanna Macy has envisioned "surveillance communities" forming around nuclear facilities, centers where the monitoring and repairing of equipment and the education of citizens would become a sacred responsibility passed down from one generation to another for many hundreds of years. I imagined a solemn ceremony taking place each year on the anniversary of the date the facility opened. We citizens would burn candles, pray and sing as we joined hands all around the 500-acre site to formalize the need for shared vigilance.

Creating such a guardianship would be difficult, maintaining it more so. I could not summon the courage to say, "I embrace the nuclear waste and will cease my fight to keep it out of my community." Yet I did determine that, once the site was chosen, I would have the courage not just to keep living here, but to treat that dump as my new neighbor. Only by doing so can I usher waste back into the circle of life. Only by cherishing the waste can I say with both conviction and experience that the whole of the Earth is beautiful and I am its caretaker.

UNCOMMON GRATITUDE

Before me lies a slope of wild grasses, saturated in the copper light of early autumn. Insects dabble in wild asters and Queen Anne's lace, and animal trails wind through the dense greenery. But just where the terrain should plunge steeply through a woodland of maple, beech, cherry, and ash trees, it flattens out like a gigantic tennis court or helicopter landing pad. What just a few weeks earlier and for many thousands of years before had been a hillside in rural northeastern Pennsylvania has been sliced in half by a five-acre concrete slab. It is, in fact, the site of a new gas pad. The next step in the process of redefining this place will be the hydrofracking that will shoot six to eight million gallons of water mixed with sand and chemicals a mile down, then horizontally through the bedrock, which, so punctured, will release its stores of natural gas.

Looking down, I can't help but feel sorry for this hill and everything associated with it: the birds and animals that lived in the woods, the water table that may be contaminated by the chemicals, the shapely hillside itself, the farm family that lives just a few hundred feet away, the soil, the rock, even the microbes that live in the rock and will receive a lethal dose of biocide to prevent them from clogging up the pipes. I also feel sorry for myself, because I take the land around me personally. I wish there were something I could do to acknowledge what's happening here, what's being taken away.

Or maybe what I want is some way to thank the place for what it gave for so long and can give no more. Or — the thought strikes with conviction, if illogic — I'd just like to cheer the place up.

The gifts a place gives to people are abundant. A list of those that my own places have provided might include:

the angle of sunrise
the creek
the trail to the peak
ripe tomatoes in the garden
neighbors
the views embraced by windows
the calls of ravens
cherry blossoms in spring
the fox prancing over the grass at dawn
sidewalks, alleys, shortcuts that know me
a tree that looks like a candelabra in the meadow
birdsong in the morning
crickets at night
the New York City skyline
stars
green grass in the backyard
green grass in the neighborhood park
sunshine on dew
moonlight on snow
the angle of sunset

When I receive a gift I am acutely conscious of both the gift and the giver, and gratitude spreads through me. This gratitude coalesces into a wish to give something back. I long to please my giver, endow that generous benefactor with something that will offer comfort, nourishment, and delight equal to what I've received. When my benefactor is a place rather than a person, however, my role as recipient is less direct. I'm someone who has inadvertently stepped beneath a stream of beneficence not specifically intended for me but suddenly pouring all over me. If I wished to offer thanks, how would I do so? Does a place have consciousness, such that it can receive gratitude for what it has given just by being itself?

People of traditional cultures would say yes, indisputably, and moreover that the expression of gratitude is not a single act taken in response to a single instance of bounty, but part of an ongoing cycle of giving and taking, taking and giving. In the late 1980s and early '90s I spent a lot of time on Navajo and Hopi lands, writing about a land dispute and relocation issue. The Navajo families I visited would make a simple prayer to the plants they wished to harvest, the sheep they were about to butcher, explaining that they intended to take from them. They assured those living beings that what they were doing was necessary for the good of the human inhabitants of the place, and expressed their hope that the plant or sheep people might continue to flourish as well. Only then would they harvest the plant, draw the knife across the throat of the sheep. The reciprocity in this simple ceremony was implicit.

Contemporary non-natives might consider such practices touching but arcane, and rather irrelevant to our own lives. Pause in gratitude for each item we drop into our cart as we rush through the supermarket after work, inventing as we go the meal we'll put together for the family dinner? Thank the rare-earth minerals invisibly melded into our smartphones every time we open an app? Not likely. Most of us are far removed from that perpetual wheel of giving and taking.

Driving through rural Pennsylvania, a friend and I pass a large farm. Spread out on a green field among an array of attractive white farm buildings with red trim are dozens of small white plastic crates. We know that inside each one a veal calf is being raised. We know, too, that these young animals were separated from their mothers immediately after they were born and that they will spend their entire short lives tied up in these crates, which are so confining the animals can't even turn around. My friend and I fall silent as the rows of crates slip past the window and disappear behind us. Eventually, we speak of how sad we feel to see animals treated like that. We affirm, as if trying to prove to each other that we're somehow addressing the problem, that we ourselves never eat veal. But we wish there were something more we could do to end their suffering.

When a beautiful place is rendered unbeautiful, when a generous place is exploited until it can give no more, when an animal is forced to endure cruel conditions, our tendency is to turn away. A polluted, disturbed, unsightly place becomes a castoff, like an old, threadbare item of clothing or a kitchen appliance that no longer works. Once a place bears this stigma of contagion, says author and University of Vermont environmental studies professor Adrian Ivakhiv, it becomes "taboo," off-limits, sometimes officially, sometimes just in the individual or collective mind. "Just as humans have set aside certain places for sacred or ritual events," Ivakhiv says, "other places have been set aside because they are too dangerous or damaged to be in contact with." Such a place seems to have lost not only its appeal but also its validity, both as a part of the physical landscape and of the psychological landscape of the human community that once valued it.

Certainly these sad, toxic, taboo places deserve as much recognition and gratitude as their unmolested counterparts. They've taken on a burden that other places have been spared. An Oneida friend of mine once compared wounded places to veterans of war. "They've given a lot," he said. "You may not agree with the war, but you have to honor the warriors."

When I consider the places I've loved and lost, I long to bring them comfort. I wish there were some way to say, *I'm sorry. I appreciate you. I want to help.* Whether in gratitude or compassion, sorrow or delight, recognition of how things used to be or consolation for what's coming, I who have been gifted by a place wish to figure out some way to return the gesture. But what kind of gift would be right for a scraped hillside slated for fracking? For calves confined to life in crates? For all the polluted rivers, clearcut forests, diminishing wildernesses, and smoldering dumps? What I seek is a gift I can offer whenever it's needed. It has to be light enough to carry and affordable enough that I can easily stock up on a large supply. It must be specific, personal, portable, and rare.

One possible answer comes to me on a backpacking trip with friends in the canyons of southeastern Utah. On a clear blue and gold morning in late spring, I leave camp and go off to explore a particularly alluring side canyon. My eyes are dipping up and down between the cliffs, where I hope to spot Anasazi ruins, and the dry wash, with its smooth stones the colors of jade, blood, and slate, when a tree moves into my line of vision. I am fully aware of it, as if it has suddenly stepped forth from its seclusion on the bank. Lightning-charred, ragged, gouged with holes, obviously a cottonwood in its former life, it demands to be reckoned with.

There is something venerable about a tree struck by lightning. Nakedly it bears its whole history: life, death, the cause of its death, and sometimes even its survival after death. I try to imagine this tree when it was alive. It must have been a formidable presence here in this stone canyon. Rabbits and deer would have sought it out for its tasty shoots, especially in the winter months, when the buds continued to develop. Many birds would have nested in the tree, and owls would have perched in it at night to watch for prey passing underneath. When branches fell off, which would have happened with increasing frequency as the tree got older, woodpeckers, bats, and even bears could have found food and shelter in the hollows. Without question, this tree gave a lot during its long life.

Impulsively I feel the urge to celebrate the abundance of gifts it gave by offering a gift of my own. From the wash I collect stones in the brightest colors I can find and ring them around the base of the tree. I pick wildflowers and place them in the holes pocking the trunk, select shapes of bleached wood and arrange them amid the stones. The bright colors stand out, jewel-like, against the shiny ebony char. When I have completed my ministrations, the tree looks resplendent enough to preside at some great ceremony. As for me, I feel I've formed a compact with this venerable being. "Sometimes it is necessary / to reteach a thing its loveliness," writes Galway Kinnell in his poem "Saint Francis and the Sow." I feel I've done much the same for this noble wreck of a cottonwood.

The discovery itself is a gift: by offering a bit of beauty to a being or place that has been felled, fracked, polluted, abused, or in some other way robbed of its dignity and purpose, I can replenish its loveliness. By believing — and then acting on — the conviction that a place is worthy of receiving some kind of gift, my consciousness shifts from anger, disgust, or sadness to one of compassion, engagement, and creativity. I realize that when my friend and I passed that veal farm, we could have stopped the car, gotten out, picked wildflowers from the roadside, and arranged them on the grass in honor of the calves. We could have sung a song or made a prayer.

Offering a gift to a damaged place is a burst of compassionate action like the splash a pebble makes when it's tossed into a pond. Only I don't ask myself where the ripples might lead; I focus on the splash. Making a spontaneous gift to a place doesn't require me to spend money, be an expert, mobilize people, or haul in supplies. No one knows I've given it, and I'll get no credit for it. Once I leave the place, the gift belongs not to posterity but to the winds, rains, and animals. Its efficacy can't be measured, but, like a kiss, a laugh, or the instinct to rush to the aid of someone who's tripped and fallen on the street, it's an impulse I agree to act on because I'm a human being seized with the urge to respond to the world around me. My gift can be a first step to further activism on an issue, but it can also be an act complete unto itself — whimsical, wild, temporary, imperfect, and wonderfully impractical.

It's now midsummer, and industrial-sized gas-drilling trucks have begun grinding up and down a graveled slope near my village. I feel the familiar heaviness and despair encroaching, but then it occurs to me that I could visit the place and see what, if anything, I might have to offer.

On a Sunday afternoon, when the crews have the day off, I slip past the no trespassing signs, duck under a metal gate, and start up the hill. The gravel road, wide enough for two trucks to pass without scraping each other, looks incongruous cutting through the mixed hardwood forest dotted with overgrown meadows. About half a mile from the main road both the hill and the gravel level off at the gas pad. A large rectangular plot has been cleared, and sheets of sticky, black, feltlike geotextile material lie over the entire area except the middle, where, a few feet above a hole about the size of a child's wading pool, pokes the gas well, neatly capped. Around the pad stand a generator; tall lighting structures; a few of the boxcarlike containers that the gas companies use to transport water from rivers and streams to drilling sites, where they mix it with fracking chemicals and sand; a port-o-john; and other pieces of equipment bespeaking the imminence of major activity. Yet all around, on the perimeters of the cleared area, life carries on as if nothing were amiss. Wild daisies, purple clover, orange hawkweed, and Queen Anne's Lace are already reclaiming the verge of the cut woods. Late afternoon sun suffuses the foliage with emerald light, and deep in the woods a hermit thrush sings its flutelike song. As I look around, a pair of bluebirds flits over the gas pad toward a tree.

There are moments when I find myself so seduced by the life of a place, carrying on in the way it must, that all I want is to abide there for a while. I want to be part clover, part maple leaf radiating sun, part song of thrush, and only enough human that I can relish and remember the experience. Yet because I can't be anything but fully human, I am unable to prevent my vigilant mind from interrupting that ravishment with knowledge of the imminent destruction of this place. I savor the moment and mourn the future, especially since the motivation for what is about to happen here is the extraction of fossil fuel to feed a world that is already cooking itself to death.

I don't know exactly what I have in mind when I step over the rolled edge of the geotextile. All I know is that I want to get closer to the reality of this newly industrialized site and my own responses to it. For a while I just wander, covering territory, looking around and looking within. Then it comes to me to form poses, something like yoga postures. First, arms outspread, body leaning forward like a masthead, I am a bluebird on the wing. Next I'm the massive metal wellhead, currently doing nothing but holding tight and waiting to be called into service. I am myself, bent over in sorrow for what will be lost when the fracking gets underway.

By now I'm swept up in this activity. Tilting forward, I plant my hands on the ground, then slide fully horizontal, like fracking liquid shooting into shale. I am a daisy turning toward the sun. I am gas bubbling through pipes, microbes flinching from the gathering biocides. Since I derive my new postures from the asanas of yoga, I name them "gasanas."

By the time I step back over the edge of my sticky, black, improvised yoga mat, I'm splotched with tarry goo, but the place itself feels different to me, less a lovely and innocent being facing a cruel future, more like a source of resilience and relentless creativity. Deep down I know it's really my attitude, not the place, that has undergone this transformation. But that itself is significant. Mourning what was, absorbing as best as I can what is, and expressing the two through a spontaneous, playful offering, I have implicated myself in the situation at hand.

I'm still unhappy about the industrial activity that has happened and will happen here. But looking around at the daisies, the woods where the thrush still sings, the gas pad that — who could have guessed it? — can easily be transformed to a performance space, I realize that I love this place. I bow in gratitude before turning to walk back down the hill.

GAZE EVEN HERE

A couple of hours past the ferry landing that links Victoria, British Columbia to Port Angeles, Washington, past the vacation area around Lake Cowichan, with its bait and tackle stores, small grocers, and cabins huddled among tall pines on the lake, the paved road ends and a rutted dirt logging road begins. Almost immediately the forest itself ends, and a clearcut breaks over us like a tsunami. There are four of us in the car, and we all get out to face it. Down the mountains and up the mountains, unrelieved except by the road that cuts through it, lie the remains of a forest. Rounds of massive trunks supply the only focal point for the eyes, while a tangle of ripped branches and limbs fills every conceivable space between them. All the way to the horizons the land has faded to gray. The place is not only dead, but mutilated. For several moments we stand there and allow ourselves to be hit, over and over, by the sight of it. When we get back into the car, shocked silence clatters behind us like a dragging muffler.

We drive on.

Aversion is a natural response to bearing witness to something tragic. "Why don't you switch channels and see if there's anything else on." That's what the husband of a friend of mine would say during those weeks in the spring of 2010, when oil from BP's Deepwater Horizon blowout was gushing into the Gulf of Mexico, and his favorite news channel showed yet another image of dying wildlife: a brown pelican struggling to raise heavy wings drenched in oil; a pod of dolphins plowing through viscous pink and blue ribbons of petroleum, expelling oil through their blowholes; a gull peering out through a thick chocolaty confection, the eye within obviously belonging to a creature who was barely alive and not likely to endure much longer. My friend's husband would make his request casually, as if he were merely curious whether something interesting might be happening on another network. The truth, she told me, was that the sight of those helpless animals made him so sad he couldn't bear to look at them.

Who among us doesn't know the feeling? Those photos were wrenching. Every time we were confronted with one, a reserve of sorrow and pity cracked open inside us, threatening to release a flood of something overwhelming. Our immediate reaction was to make the whole situation go away: turn the channel, turn the page, click to a different page of the internet. In the weeks following the spill, however, I began to wonder whether relief might lie not in looking away, but in deliberately turning our attention to those suffering creatures.

According to Francis Ponge, the early-twentieth-century French poet and chronicler of the mythic existence of ordinary things, we cannot truly see something until we allow it to "disarrange" us. Ponge advocated a manner of regarding the world's constituents not as inferiors that we must somehow corral for our use and understanding, but as equals capable of startling us with the marvel of their particular selfhood. To a busy, focused adult negotiating life today, Ponge's advice may sound naïve, romantic. To allow ourselves to be disarranged by things would be to concede to a kind of helplessness, would it not? Instead of penetrating the world, ever pushing ourselves forth with the great engine of human intention that, we believe, enables us to control, organize, manage, and cope, we would, if we took Ponge's advice, submit to being penetrated ourselves.

Of course, whether we're aware of it or not, we do consent, and willingly, to such visual penetration many times throughout the day. The world thrusts itself upon us, and we take heed. We're driving, walking through a parking lot, eating in a restaurant, working at our desk when something suddenly swoops in, grabs us, and yanks us in its direction, and we can't help but follow. Someone beautiful walks into a room, a waiter drops a tray, a colleague taps on the office door. Then we're momentarily disarranged as curiosity takes over. Sometimes the interruption is so out of the ordinary that we wish to look longer, to give ourselves over to soaking up the surprise — to stare. But staring is rude. When we were children, our mothers hissed at us and jerked our arms when they caught us staring at some fascinating human who looked different from anyone we'd ever seen. As adults, well trained, we look quickly away if we're caught staring, pretending that our focus was but passing over the other and would never, ever linger. Staring is hungry. It wants more and more. It invades the polite space that is supposed to separate us from others. When the starer is caught, it's he, not the stared-at, who's exposed.

Another means of prolonged looking, the gaze is different from the stare. Gazing is the occupation of babies and lovers, some museum goers, and those who take advantage of scenic overlooks on highways. Babies don't know the world well enough to discern the anomaly in the familiar; it's all a wonder to them. The look through which they explore this mystery is open, receptive. It takes in the whole environment, available for whatever may appear. The gaze brushes its subject; the stare pierces. Later in life, when we bring the gaze to love, we offer it up as the doorway through which we can enter the mysterious depths of the other, while being similarly entered. The stare wants to sneak in without being spotted; the gaze has nothing to hide and assumes the other is equally accessible and open. This softening into the enchantment of the other is what Roland Barthes calls the "exaltation of loving *someone unknown*, someone who will remain so forever: a mystic impulse."

The gaze is demanding; you can't just schedule a few minutes for it in the midst of a busy day. You have to settle in with a gaze, as with a cocktail. If the stare gulps, the gaze sips.

Of course, the invitation to gaze is typically issued by what pleases the eyes, not by what affronts them. The man who asked his wife to turn the channel felt assaulted when the TV news forced him to consider images of wildlife tortured by oil. It's no wonder he wanted to get away. Not only is it painful to look at a suffering animal, but we're not used to having that kind of demand made on our sensibilities by the public media. In fact, we're generally discouraged from feeling pity for the nonhuman.

Those who do call attention to the plight of a plant or a nondomestic animal may be derided as a tree-hugger, someone who cares more about owls (or fish or moss or beetles) than people. She may be accused of indulging in that ultimate form of mushy thinking, anthropomorphism.

Calling attention to suffering or about-to-suffer wildlife is typically the work of environmental and animal rights groups. The photographs they include with their appeals for donations make us confront either a present horror (dogs and cats with wires and boxes attached to their living, flayed bodies) or an imminent danger (baby seals basking on a rock, presumably as a boatload of hunters rounds a nearby iceberg). The minute you look at those pictures, you know what is being demanded of you: horror, outrage, and the near simultaneous impulse to make those feelings go away. You don't even need to read the accompanying text. You're already sufficiently appalled, predisposed to agree that something must be done, and to trust the people who have disseminated the picture to know what that something is. All you have to do is write a check or type in your credit card number and click SEND. These campaigns make you look, but they protect you from having to look for very long.

Poet Gary Snyder has expressed his desire for a new branch of ecology, one that would force us to consider the "dark side of nature — the ball of crunched bones in a scat, the feathers in the snow, the tales of insatiable appetite." I imagine students of such a course in the grim, gruesome, and visceral taking notes as they watch vultures tear into the flesh of a deer lying dead on a highway. They would ponder examples of nature's perversity, like blight and mutation or the fat male macaque I once, yes, stared at in guilty fascination in a remote temple on Bali. In one gray paw he was dragging around an emaciated yellow cat, which he would remonstratively whack against the stone floor every time it struggled weakly, after which declaration of authority he would squat down and peer casually about his realm.

But the dark side of nature must also include those species and places that have been darkened by the insatiable appetites of the human race. In some ways we humans are like that macaque, only it's the wild places we love that we're beating into submission. You know the ones I mean.

Those places that were as much a part of you as your family and your own private thoughts. Those places where you could lose yourself and find yourself at the same time. Those places that had the power to enchant you every time you, like a lover, entered their mystery. You may think you've accepted their disappearance, convinced yourself of the indomitableness of progress, and gotten over the loss, but they're still there, residing in you, though you can no longer visit them. They linger, laden with emotion in your memory, and they hover like ghosts right there in the world where they used to be, even though other things have taken their place. They're there behind the "beauty strip," that neat scrim of tall trees left on the highway to fool you into thinking that a forest, rather than a wasteland of clearcutting, extends back over the hills. They're those scars you can almost see in the sky, tracing the shape of what for millions of years was the Appalachian skyline, now flattened since the mountaintops have been detonated to facilitate coal mining. They're in the waves still lapping at the beaches where you no longer take your children, because toxic waste fouls the water. They're underneath the dead rivers, the filthy horizon, the dying ash and hemlock and pinyon trees, the meadows paved over, the silence over the roses that bees no longer visit, the twilight sky emptied of bats. The dark side of nature seeps into your memory and imagination, reminding you not just of what the place used to be, but what you, too, used to be when it was part of you.

Glenn Albrecht, a philosopher and professor of sustainability at Murdoch University in Perth, Australia, has coined a term, *solastalgia*, to define the psychological impact on people when the world they know is damaged. Derived from the Latin word *solacium* (comfort) and the Greek root *algia* (pain), solastalgia means "the pain experienced when there is recognition that the place where one resides and that one loves is under immediate assault." We are victims of solastalgia not when we leave our home, Albrecht points out, but when our home leaves us. So what can a person do besides write letters to the editor and give money to the good guys who promise to do at least something to fix it? Turn the channel? Move? Suck it up and tell yourself that this is progress and inevitable?

Rant to your friends, all the while believing yourself powerless to change anything? Or, perhaps, deliberately turn to that broken, wasted place and gaze at it.

Upon entering the clearcut on Vancouver Island, we did not drive on to some prettier, greener place. We drove straight into the heart of it and stayed for several days.

On our first morning, we developed a routine and a question. The routine consisted of having breakfast together in the primitive campground at the end of the road, part of a forty-thousand-acre fragment of old-growth forest that lies at the western edge of the clearcut, where eight-hundred-year-old Sitka spruces and cedars tower over deep, soft moss and primeval ferns. Then we made our lunches and set off together up the dirt road where, just a quarter mile from the campground, the forest ended abruptly and the land opened into thousands of square miles of clearcut. There we separated, each to spend the day alone in the logged area. In the evening we regathered in the campground, cooked and ate dinner, then made our way to a gigantic spruce, where we told the stories of what we had experienced during the day.

The question was this: what would happen if we simply settled into this damaged place, observing the land and our own responses to it? Our intention was to get to know this place that we had heartily wished to run from.

I chose to spend every day in the same spot, sitting on the same big stump. The waist-high debris was so thick and treacherous that it took ten minutes to negotiate the twenty-foot distance from the road, since I had to hold on to protruding limbs and step with care to avoid plunging three jagged feet down. Once I arrived, however, I had a place to sit and take it all in. On the first morning the bleak reality of the situation left room for no other reaction but sorrow, but gradually something else took over. You could call it fascination. Details of the place started emerging: the color of the bark, the pattern of the rings in the trunk I nested on. Almost immediately upon arriving on that first day I heard a bird singing close by and was momentarily amazed that a bird could find something to sing about in such a place. Later I discovered that I could lie down on my tree stump and be supported from the top of my head down to my calves. I confess that at that moment I experienced what could only be described as glee. I began to wonder how long it actually took an eight-hundred-year-old tree to die. Perhaps it did not die all at once, as a person or animal would if its upper half were lopped off; perhaps life ebbed slowly from a tree. I peered at insects eating through the wood and had to recognize their contentment at the state of things. Once, just sitting and gazing, I spotted a mother black bear and two cubs making their way as deftly as acrobats over the wreckage no more than thirty feet from my perch.

The practice of gazing on the wounded forest evoked a consciousness of brokenness in our personal lives. One woman was struck by how the land mirrored her own wasted youth, and the inescapability of the destruction all around enabled her to grieve for both the forest and her own past in a way that had never before seemed possible. She started making altars on the stumps, first for her own youth, then for the forest, and eventually for those she thought of as the destroyers — the loggers, the consumers, the people she had previously been unable to forgive. One of the men realized that the practice of sitting on a stump and gazing hour after hour at the wreckage of the forest was something he could bring back home to his troubled marriage. He saw that he was always looking for excuses to flee the house, instead of sitting down with his wife long enough to discuss their problems. He determined that, when he got back home, he would be present with her, and with the marriage, the way he was learning to be present with the forest.

That the landscape around us would mirror the landscape within was not surprising to our group. Each of us had been involved with wilderness rites of passage programs, either as guides or participants. We knew that when a person spends time alone in a wild place, allowing aspects of the land to provoke fascination, desire, grief, or repulsion then probing his own responses, a subtle but illuminating dialogue begins. Perceiving how the natural world feeds, flees, dies, lets go, puts out thorns, and manifests countless other ways of prevailing, we are inspired not just by the tenacity of nature, but by the way that such tactics seem applicable to our own lives and circumstances. We see nature more clearly, but we also notice new things about ourselves. However, these sorts of journeys typically occur in unspoiled mountains, deserts, and canyons. Deliberately seeking out a damaged place was something else entirely.

Slowly, we came to realize that our practice of purposefully seeking meaning and beauty in the wounded was teaching us important lessons about wholeness. We saw how life survived in this forest of stumps. We realized that the denizens of the place did not consider their habitat wounded; they merely coped and adapted. We understood on a visceral level that what is ugly, broken, and decaying is part of the whole. That truth granted us more acceptance of the broken, ugly, decaying aspects of ourselves. The clearcut also opened new reserves of compassion in each of us. When we first arrived, we regarded as villains the lumberjacks who had toppled these ancient and venerable trees. Before long we realized that they, and even the corporations they worked for, were merely supplying all of us members of the consumer culture with the products we constantly demanded, from toilet paper to airline boarding passes to some critically acclaimed new book about climate change. We saw that we were all part of the problem and that we were all victims of a process much larger than ourselves.

Gazing at the clearcut enabled an exchange between people and place. We brought our attention, curiosity, and openness to the place, and it, in turn, provided us with inspiration, compassion, and, yes, beauty. We discovered that what we had feared would be too painful to bear was not. Gradually, by practicing the art of gazing, we got to know this broken forest. And then, so slowly we hardly recognized what was happening, we began to love the place. There is no other way to say this. Willingness to look turned into curiosity, which turned into acceptance, which turned into compassion, and that turned into love. By the end of the week, none of us wanted to leave.

Buddhists call the practice of looking fixedly at something "sustaining the gaze." When one sustains the gaze during meditation, she regards a thing, whether outside or within herself, with emotional detachment, open to what it might reveal about itself, her, or the world. Her intention in such gazing is to bypass ordinary ways of looking, which are weighted with critical judgment, predatory appraisal *(how can this feed me, how can I use it?)*, or fracturing through the need to categorize *(where shall I file this in my mind?)*. The model gazers in Buddhist iconography are the Buddha himself and the goddess Kuan Yin. They gaze at the human condition, taking in what is there in all its thorny complexity, while maintaining a smooth, openhearted compassion.

Sustaining the gaze, the meditator looks without trying to fix. That's hard, maybe especially hard for Americans, since our cultural mythos is grounded in our can-do attitude, our conviction that "if you put your mind to it, you can accomplish anything." Can we merely absorb devastation, even for a few minutes, offering acceptance and compassion, or is that un-American? Aren't you supposed to repair what's broken? Or, failing to repair, shouldn't you get right back up on the horse that threw you and gallop once more into the fray? A man who heads one of the country's leading environmental organizations told me recently that when the massive efforts of one of his teams fail to pay off, when they aren't able to save a forest or canyon, or species of tree or fish after putting their hearts, time, and energy into the project for months and even years, there is no recourse for expressing regret or sorrow. Instead, "We pretty much turn our backs on it and put all our energy into the next project," he said. "We can't wallow."

But when you consider all the loved places, plants, and animals that vanish, more and more every year, don't you feel you owe them something? Maybe you can't save them — you can't reconstruct those mountaintops or green the gray, ragged forests or seed the twilight sky with bats — but isn't some kind of acknowledgment of their current state only right? You don't abandon a friend when he gets sick. You go to his bedside, hold his hand, and accept what has befallen him, even though you wish so badly that things were otherwise it almost breaks your heart.

Above all, you keep loving him. So, too, must we continue to love those places, trees, and animals, for we have a relationship with them as well. They're not the places we remember, but they are still alive, and they can still offer us beauty, refuge, and delight. They infuse us with amazement for a world bigger and more mysterious than the human, and they remind us that we, too, are part of that mystery.

That's why, when the media was broadcasting all those images of suffering wildlife in the Gulf, I knew I had to look. It seemed the least I could do. Unlike a Buddhist, I didn't seek detachment. Just the opposite: I was aiming to connect, the way I had in the clearcut. I wanted to absorb, as best I could, both the sight before me and my own response to it, and to take up a bit of the burden. So, every time I encountered a photo or video, I made a practice of choosing to gaze at it. And, frankly, nearly every first glance brought a kick of revulsion. In the clearcut, we had confronted a place that was already destroyed; the oil-smothered beings in these images still had blood, brains, mobility, intent. This gull, plastered in black oil, sprawled on a beach, oil dripping off its head and wings, webbed feet slicked and splayed, its bright eye still filled with enough life to peer at the human with his camera, who has come closer than the bird would ever allow if it could resist, but cannot resist because it is dying: I did not want to encounter it. Step one, committing to the gaze, never got easier.

After a moment, though, the revulsion melted enough to expose rough sorrow just below. The sorrow lasted longer. Like a spotlight, it fixed first on that particular bird and then spread, gathering into its beam all the lives now being spoiled by this surge of oil into water — the microorganisms obligingly eating the poison before them, the marsh grass drooping in the bayous, the turtles, the fishermen with their beached boats, unable to fish, the fish. The families who relied on the fish for their suppers. I sat there encased in despair the way that bird was encased in oil. Then, as had happened regularly in the clearcut, my mind would up and decide it had had enough. I'd start thinking about a phone call that hadn't gone well, or how I was going to end a certain piece of writing, and then, urgently, I'd conclude that this exercise was done.

Every time I resisted the urge to quit, however, and made the choice to keep looking, what I met with felt a little less caustic, a little more familiar. *Hello, bird, I'm back.*

Sometimes, unpredictably, through the sorrow pierced a shaft of joy. Outrageous, to be sure, but it was joy, no doubt about it. Joy burst forth through the pervading gloom like life determined to prevail. Life was in the eye of that gull that, despite imminent death, maintained its own fierce gaze. Life was in the pelican struggling to lift its oil-drenched wings and fly. Life was in people you kept hearing about in the news, reaching beyond their desperation to help others. I, by committing to the gaze, became both part of the predicament and part of life's tenacious drive to hold on as long and fiercely as possible.

But whether joy arrived at the end of a spell of looking or not, a change always occurred, and it went something like this: I had ventured into a place I had preferred to avoid, and in the journey encountered the monsters of revulsion, avoidance, and despair. They had not destroyed me, though. For a few moments, I had abided with them in a reality too big to change, but too pressing to ignore, and eventually, as happens to every monster in myth and fairy tale, they had transformed into something beautiful.

LAMENT AND PRAISE FOR THE EARTH

This blue and white orb that *Voyager* spacecraft revealed, shimmering like a jewel among the vast dark bands of space, this planet that's been greening for 500 million years, this tumult of ingenuity, this bed of desire, mass of ambitions, playing field of gods — it all began as a great ball of fire. Earth congealed from a spinning ball of hot rock. A mere 4.6 billion years later, it teems with life.

An essential part of this complex thing called life is the ability of living beings to assess their circumstances and readjust them. River, wooly mammoth, malaria mosquito, house cat, Cleopatra, Ringo Starr, ruby-throated hummingbird, you and me — we all chafe at some conditions of our world and strive to make things more to our liking. One species among all the billions that have existed has gotten the entire planet into a terrible mess. Earth began as heat, and now we face the loss of much we love on our home planet, because we have overloaded it with heat.

How on Earth are we going to meet this crisis? Already some animals and plants are making biological adjustments to survive a hotter future. The beaks of Australian parrots, for example, have increased ten percent in size since 1871 because of a process called Allen's Rule, which dictates that certain parts of an animal's body become larger, so that they can evaporate heat over a greater area. Other species, like a pink salmon in Alaska, which now migrates two weeks earlier than previously, adapt by shifting the timing of their life cycles. Some animals, such as moose, frogs, and thousands of others, are moving farther north.

But how will we humans evolve? I can do my sustainable part by buying local foods, checking books out of the library instead of ordering them online, flying less. But how will I cope emotionally? Spiritually? How will any of us cope? How are we to respond to this unprecedented calamity? How can we live with the seismic shifting of ancient balances, the demise of so much life, the erosion of hope and expectations among young people? I know I cannot run away. I must face all that is happening and I must lament. Grief, after all, is appropriate in times of great loss. And yet, if I just pay attention, I can also praise this broken, beautiful world. I can find and make beauty, not despite the ravages of climate change, but in the very midst of them. And then, I believe, I can survive.

For every bit of life on Earth that I lament, I can — I *must* — find some way to praise.

Lament and praise for the land that holds us

The land that holds us is the entire composition of a place we love, physical and metaphysical, present and past, outside our bodies and inside our hearts. It is the long rim on the horizon where the sun rises and sinks throughout the seasons. The land that holds us is the waters, the hills, all those shortcuts we've found, the smell of lilac in the spring and chlorine in the public pool in summer. It is the sounds — roosters, motorbikes, calls to prayer, and, everywhere, children playing. The land is the memories that arise from bends in the road and the walls in houses. It is the people who move among these familiar forms.

Climate change now endangers the land that holds us, no matter where we live. As for me, I worry not only about the fierce winds that disarrange trees and down power lines, but also about the droughts, wildfires, heat, and tornadoes my friends are facing in their loved lands. Several have emergency bags packed for a quick escape. Some have already lost their homes. A woman I met sank into prolonged grief when wildfires destroyed the California home where she, her husband, and their children had lived for more than twenty years. That heavy burden began to lighten on the day she walked over the land with a friend. All the grieving woman saw was char and loss. But her friend saw something else. She would pause often to exclaim over green sprouts poking through the ash or point out the call of a varied thrush. "She was teaching me to see what was there," said the grieving woman, "not what was missing, which was just a wonderful gift."

Lament and praise for the inability to fix it

When hurricanes, floods, or wildfires collapse a town, few citizens are deterred from optimism once the shock of the loss begins to fade. They declare their determination to pluck themselves up, band together, and rebuild their community "back to normal." Refusing to let tragedy conquer us is vital to the human spirit. But can we really fix, or even ameliorate, the many calamities of climate change, or must we start practicing a new form of acceptance?

"I accept the universe," declared the nineteenth century author and feminist Margaret Fuller. "Gad, she'd better," sarcastically quipped philosopher Thomas Carlyle. But William James understood what Fuller meant. In his response to Carlyle, reprinted in *The Varieties of Religious Experience*, he wrote, "If we accept the whole, shall we do so as if stunned into submission… or shall we do so with enthusiastic assent?"

Enthusiastic assent? How do I accept the unacceptable? How am I to accept that storms and fires will get worse, animal species will become extinct, and all over the world desperate people will be displaced?

To accept a situation is to accept that it is happening, not that it is right. Acceptance of circumstances is the first step to dealing with them. Hospice director and author Steven Levine wrote that there often comes a point when a terminally ill person realizes that they must seek a different kind of healing, one intended not to repair a failing body, but rather to heal family relationships, embrace a new spirituality, or find long-delayed forgiveness of self or other. Accepting climate change means I fully acknowledge the reality of an unprecedented and frightening phenomenon. And it is my very inability to "fix" the problem that can open up for me countless opportunities to become more attentive to the grace of the present, more compassionate, and shrewder about the choices I make. I cannot fix the future, yet I can utterly transform the present. Acceptance does not mean submission.

Lament and praise for the mystery of animal nations

In my backyard, a small clump of purple beebalm has become an insect supermarket. I dug a few stalks from the garden of my previous home and replanted them here, but until now the plant has languished. Suddenly, it blooms, and its blooms beckon.

Yet my very exhilaration over the activity of a few insects on a few flowers saddens me, for I can't help remembering the bee-life during summers when my husband and I rented a cabin on a lake in northeastern Pennsylvania. On one side of the dirt driveway ran a wall of rose bushes, and when the blossoms arrived, bees of all nations gathered. The communal buzzing was so loud we could hear it from inside the cabin thirty feet away. Kinetic with insect intention, the small white roses seemed to wriggle of their own accord.

Henry Beston wrote of animals, "They are not brethren, they are not underlings; they are other nations, caught with ourselves in the net of life and time." Now these nations are under grave threat. Biologists estimate that up to 35 percent of plants and animals alive today could become extinct by 2050. Animals are our ancestors, and they have modeled for us many miraculous ways of getting things done in their environments. They teach us humans what plants are good to eat and which to ingest as medicine. They demonstrate how to be attentive, patient, creative, and cunning.

A Diné (Navajo) friend told me about the gift a porcupine gave her grandmother. The woman had to walk a long way from her hogan to the spring to get water for the family. One day she heard a plaintive cry. When she went to investigate, she found a porcupine trapped between two rocks. She freed the animal, and when it sauntered off, it led her to a source of water much closer to her home. Even if we never receive such a direct gift, animal presence engages and enthralls us, from the polar bear most of us will never encounter to the cricket singing under the porch at night.

Gratefully I will take whatever I get. So out I go yet again to watch those few bees feasting at my flowers.

Lament and praise for the companionship of seasons

On a sheet of papyrus, a poet of Egypt's New Kingdom (1550-1080 BC) compared his passion for his beloved with the rhythms of the seasons: "All the trees except / for me have shed their leaves / in the meadow. Only I / flower all year in the garden." For millennia, the emergences and losses of the seasons have not only informed us when to plant and harvest crops, they've also provided insights about the ways of the gods and mirrors of the human heart. Three thousand years later, we confront an "ecological mismatch," in the words of British scientist Ulf Büntgen. "It means," he wrote, "that millions of years of careful mapping that has allowed plants, birds, and insects to find and co-exist with one another, is drastically off, and becoming more so." Now our poems turn to elegies, for as rapper Childish Gambino mourns "Every day gets hotter than the one before / Running out of water, it's about to / go down / Air that kill the bees that we depend on / Birds were made for singing / Waking up to no sound."

How can I attentively mark these unpredictable and alarming shifts? Around the world, ceremonies of the seasons have brought people into intimate relationship with the cosmos, the divine, their human community, and their own place on Earth. The ancient Egyptians greeted the annual flooding of the Nile by offering gifts to the river. From classical Greece to Medieval Europe, men and women sought to encourage the fertility of the land with festivals of ribaldry, excess, and lusty coupling. On the Hopi mesas, masked kachinas even today dance into the plazas, singing and shaking rattles, to make prayers for rain that will nourish the corn. Can I create rituals to honor the seasons as they arise, even in their cockeyed form? Can I open my arms to the snowflakes that swirl briefly in the air before dissipating? Walking in the dry bed of what once was a lake, can I pause to make a symbolic offering of water from my bottle? If so, may I become more observant, more grateful, more in communion with what is.

Lament and praise for the beloved faraway

We don't have to actually go to a place for it to matter to us. People who have never been to the Arctic wilderness or the Amazon rainforest, and never will go, react indignantly to incursions of oil drilling and deforestation in those places. We need the vastness of the unknown, simply because it is unknown. It allures. American artist and writer Roni Horn is constantly being drawn back to Iceland. Experiencing unseen places, she writes, has enormous consequence for our psyche: "We need them as a way of balancing what is with what might be, and as a way of understanding the scope of things — of admitting that the things beyond us are also the things that define us. These are places that are both actual and acts of imagination. They function to keep the world large, hopeful, and unknown."

Now, tourists try to get to distant, enchanting places before they vanish and in their eagerness bring fumes, footprints, and waste that hasten the very force they're trying to outpace. At the same time, instant access to news delivers detailed information about earthquakes, floods, and fires around the world and their impact on the people who live there. I dream of a network of people who can respond creatively to such crises without doing further harm. It could be called, after Amnesty International's Urgent Action Network, the "Urgent Beauty Network." A friend of mine undertook such an action after the 2011 tsunami and the collapse of the Fukushima nuclear plant. He wrote out copies of a poem by Basho, the seventeenth century Japanese poet:

> If you will let me
> I will willingly wipe
> Salt tears from your eyes
> With these fresh leaves.

He then went round his London neighborhood and tied the poems to the blossoming cherry trees. People would have seen them. Surely they would have known what was intended by this message, gracing a species of tree for which Japan is famous. This small act did not come to the aid of suffering people far away, but it was an outward and visible expression of compassion for the beloved faraway.

Lament and praise for the ways we took for granted

In his 1836 essay, "Nature," Ralph Waldo Emerson remarked confidently that nature is so much bigger and grander than us mere humans that our influence on it could never be more than "insignificant." Almost two hundred years later, we recognize how wrong he was. I miss assuming that nature will get along fine without me. Like most of humanity, I had taken for granted that, despite wars, rebellions, social and geological upheavals, and billions of births and deaths, the Earth would continue, reliably, to be the Earth. Species would adapt. Humans would evolve. The seasons would continue to usher one another forth. This rare planet would always remain our marvelously habitable home.

It's not just the biology and meteorology of life that I have taken for granted and now risk losing. I have also taken for granted so much of what modern society has made possible, like buying with a click a new dress or the book someone recommended to me just moments earlier. I took for granted the delight of flying and gazing at Earth from the air, as if airplanes were magical conveyances, rather than major polluters. I took for granted the technology that makes possible my phone, my heat, gas pumps and email, avocados and mangos in my New York supermarket.

I weep for all that seemed possible and now is eroding and that erodes even more for those who were born in the generations after me. I weep for a future that held promise. I weep for the all lives, miniscule and great, whose grave challenges and slow vanishing I can understand intellectually but in no way prevent.

To accept the reality of climate change is to lament. That's natural. It takes a little more effort to accept that, even here there is much to praise. The Earth goes on: creating, adapting, blooming, struggling, surviving. That much is certain. And even in the midst of so much loss, new friends and collaborations will form. People will fall in love. Creativity, ingenuity, heroism, and bravery will startle and inspire. Some jobs will become obsolete, while others will bring exciting possibilities, On a personal level, I will fine-tune my attachment to the world. I will be attentive to what we are losing, in person if possible, symbolically if not, and honor it with the kind of mindful, grateful love I would bring to the bedside of a dear friend who is critically ill. I will widen my senses to what remains and give thanks for its stubborn and creative endurance. I will expect, every day, to be amazed.

SOME SOURCES FOR THE ESSAYS

WHERE'S THE TEMPLE?

2   *Jung on "divine curiosity":* C.G. Jung, *The Archetypes and the Collective Unconscious,* trans. R.F.C. Hull (New York: Princeton University Press, 1990).

3   *Caravaggio's troubling realism:* Will Wlizlo, "The Art Sleuth," *Utne Reader,* February 24, 2011.

4   *Krishna's vision of Arjuna: The Bhagavad-Gita,* trans. Barbara Stoler Miller (New York: Bantam Books, 1986), Chapter 11, Verse 30, line 103.

4   *George Smith and The Epic of Gilgamesh:* Paul Jordan-Smith, "Living Stories," *Parabola,* Vol. XI, No. 4, November 1986.

5   *"visibility is the truth":* John Berger, *The Sense of Sight* (New York: Vintage Books, 1985).

5   *vision can change:* Laura Sewall, *Sight and Sensibility: The Ecopsychology of Perception* (New York: Jeremy Tarcher, 1999).

6   *Speaking about hanblecheyapi:* Black Elk, through Joseph Epes Brown, "Hanblecheyapi: Crying for a Vision," *Teachings from the Earth: Indian Religion and Philosophy,* ed. Dennis Tedlock and Barbara Tedlock (New York: Liveright Publishing, 1975).

WITNESS TO A LANDSCAPE

9   *Heisenberg's Uncertainty Principle:* Books I love on the philosophy of quantum physics include Fritjof Capra, *The Tao of Physics;* Fred Alan Wolf, *The Spiritual Universe: One Physicist's Vision of Spirit, Soul, Matter, and Self;* and Gary Zukav, *The Dancing Wu Li Masters: An Overview of the New Physics.*

10   *"The secret of the world":* Ralph Waldo Emerson, "Fate," *Selected Essays, Lectures, and Poems* (New York: Washington Square Press, 1972).

YARDS

16   *"over-the-back-fence socializing":* William H. Whyte, "How the New Suburbia Socializes," in *The Essential William H. Whyte,* ed. Albert LaFarge (New York: Fordham University Press, 2000).

THE COAL REMEMBERS

I am grateful to Dan Werner, mining engineer at the Bureau of Abandoned Mine Reclamation in Wilkes-Barre, PA, who opened up maps of the old coal mines, sent me photos and documents, and answered many questions.

For this essay, I read many articles online. Especially informative was Paul A. Shackel, "Anthracite Heritage: Landscape, Memory and the Environment," Open Rivers website, Summer 2017.

38   *Yeats poem:* "The Circus Animals' Desertion."

DROUGHT

61 *"the primary mode of divine presence"*: Thomas Berry, *The Dream of the Earth* (San Francisco: Sierra Club Books, 1988).

62 Vine Deloria, *God Is Red: A Native View of Religion* (Golden, CO: Fulcrum Publishing, 2003).

65 Carolyn Merchant, *The Death of Nature* (New York: HarperCollins, 1989).

THE JUNIPER TREE

71 *Inuit song:* Inuit, "Magic Words (after Nalungiaq)," *Shaking the Pumpkin: Traditional Poetry of the Indian North Americans*, ed. Jerome Rothenberg (New York: Alfred van der Marck Editions, 1986).

72 *a herder who was struck by the trunk:* Carl Safina, *Beyond Words: What Animals Think and Feel* (New York: Picador Books, 2015).

72 *work with wildlife, rather than managing it:* M.J. Barrett, Viktoria Hinz, Vanessa Wijngaarden, and Marie Lovrod, "Speaking with other animals through intuitive interspecies communication: towards cognitive and interspecies justice," *A Research Agenda for Animal Geographies,* Elgaronline, January 2021.

73 Suzanne Simard, *Finding the Mother Tree: Discovering the Wisdom of the Forest* (New York: Vintage Press, 2022).

73 Masaru Emoto, *The Hidden Messages in Water* (Portland, OR: Beyond Words Publishing, 2004).

73 *"We like to think of it as a voice"*: JoAnna Klein, "Taking the Pulse of a Sandstone Tower in Utah," *The New York Times* online, September 9, 2019.

74 *the composition of the soul:* Christian Wertenbaker, "The Materiality of the Soul," *Parabola*, Vol. 37, No. 4, Winter 2012-13.

DEVOTING

76 *"The gates of hell…":* I wrote an article that included descriptions of our tour to toxic communities near New Orleans. Trebbe Johnson, "The Second Creation Story," *Sierra*, November-December, 1998.

78 *aspects of the mystical experience:* William James, *The Varieties of Religious Experience,* (New York: New American Library, 1958).

79 *even those who don't believe in it:* Barbara Ehrenreich, *Living with a Wild God: A Nonbeliever's Search for the Truth about Everything* (New York: Twelve, 2014).

80 *"all of life is a gathering up of soul":* Eliezer Shore, "Through a Dark Passage," *Parabola*, Vol. 21, No. 2, Summer 1996.

80 *the Dalai Lama was scheduled to speak:* See Trebbe Johnson, "World Religions Get Down to Earth: A Report from the 2009 Parliament of the World's Religions," *Parabola*, Vol. 35, No. 2, Summer 2010.

DRUNK WITH VIRTUE

92 *a translation of Baudelaire:* The poem Danny and I were reading was "Drunk with Virtue," in *An Anthology of French Poetry from Nerval to Valery in English Translation,* ed. Angel Flores (Garden City, NY: Anchor Books, 1958).

TRAVEL IN A DANGEROUS COUNTRY

99 *"travel in a dangerous country"*: Richard Selzer, "The Knife," in *The Art of the Personal Essay: An Anthology from the Classical Era to the Present*, ed. Phillip Lopate (New York: Anchor Books, 1994).

101 *"fierce consciousness"*: Robinson Jeffers, "Rock and Hawk."

105 *a sparrow alit on his shoulder*: Henry David Thoreau, *Walden* (London: J.M. Dent & Sons Ltd., 1943).

106 *"the innate tendency to focus"*: E.O. Wilson, *Biophilia: The Human Bond with Other Species* (Cambridge: Harvard University Press, 1984).

CARING FOR THE WASTE

120 *According to David Powless:* David Powless is an Oneida engineer who received a National Science Foundation grant to recycle steel waste. I interviewed him in 1987 for a special multimedia production for IBM. When he told me how he had realized that the steel waste was "not an enemy to be conquered, but an orphan that had gotten separated from the circle of life," I was deeply inspired. Those words led me to write my book, *Radical Joy for Hard Times: Finding Meaning and Making Beauty in Earth's Broken Places,* and also to found a nonprofit dedicated to finding and making beauty in wounded places. I tell the story of David's and my meeting and what ensued in *Radical Joy for Hard Times.*

121 *"surveillance communities"*: The late Joanna Macy wrote and spoke widely on her proposal that nuclear guardianship groups ought to form where nuclear power plants and waste facilities are located. To the best of my knowledge, the only one that currently exists is at Rocky Flats, Colorado, a former nuclear weapons manufacturing site that was extremely toxic. Although it has supposedly been

cleaned up, and wildlife has returned, the Nuclear Guardianship group is working to warn people of ongoing danger.

UNCOMMON GRATITUDE

125   *"taboo," off limits:* I heard Adrian Ivakhiv interviewed by Krista Tippet on her program, *On Being* and had a phone conversation with him in February 2009.

126   Galway Kinnell, "Saint Francis and the Sow."

GAZE EVEN HERE

131   *we allow it to "disarrange" us:* Nancy Willard, *Testimony of the Invisible Man: William Carlos Williams, Francis Ponge, Rainier Maria Rilke, Pablo Neruda* (Columbia: University of Missouri Press, 1970).

132   *"exaltation of loving someone unknown,":* Roland Barthes, *A Lover's Discourse,* trans. Richard Howard (New York: Hill and Wang, 1979).

133   *"the dark side of nature":* Gary Snyder, "Blue Mountains Walking," *The Practice of the Wild* (New York: North Point Press, 1990).

134   solastalgia, *to define the psychological impact on people:* Daniel B. Smith, "Is There an Ecological Unconscious?", *New York Times Magazine,* January 27, 2009.

LAMENT AND PRAISE FOR THE EARTH

141   *Allen's Rule, which dictates that certain parts of an animal's body become larger:* Sara Ryding and Matthew Symonds, "Animals are changing their body shapes to cope with climate change," World Economic Forum, Sept. 13, 2021

143   *"I accept the universe":* William James, *The Varieties of Religious Experience* (New York: Mentor Books, 1958).

144   *"They are not brethren":* Quoted in Carl Safina, *Beyond Words: What Animals Think and Feel* (New York: Henry Holt and Company, 2015).

145   *"All the trees / except for me":* Poem Twenty-eight, "The Orchard," in *Love Lyrics of Ancient Egypt,* trans. Barbara Hughes Fowler (Chapel Hill: The University of North Carolina Press, 1994).

145   *an "ecological mismatch:* Margaret Osborne, "Plants Are Blossoming a Month Early in the U.K. Because of Climate Change," *Smithsonian Magazine,* February 4, 2022.

145   *"Every day gets hotter":* Childish Gambino, "Feels Like Summer," YouTube.

146   *Experiencing unseen places:* Roni Horn, *Island Zombie: Iceland Writings* (Princeton: Princeton University Press, 2020).

146   *"If you will let me":* Basho, *The Narrow Road to the Deep North and Other Travel Sketches,* trans. Nobuyuki Yuasa (Harmondsworth, Middlesex, England: Penguin Books Ltd., 1966).

147   *In his 1836 essay:* Ralph Waldo Emerson, "Nature." I have a very old edition of Emerson's *Complete Essays,* so old it has no copyright. This is one of Emerson's most famous essays and is widely available, including online.

About the Author

Trebbe Johnson is also the author of *Fierce Consciousness: Surviving the Sorrows of Earth and Self*, *Radical Joy for Hard Times: Finding Meaning and Making Beauty in Earth's Broken Places*, and other books, as well as many articles and essays that explore the human bond with nature. She is also the founder of the global community Radical Joy for Hard Times, devoted to finding and making beauty in wounded places. Trebbe speaks five languages; camped alone in the Arctic wilderness; studied classical Indian dance; and worked as an artist's model, a street sweeper in an English village, and an award-winning multimedia producer. She has led contemplative journeys in a clear-cut forest, Ground Zero in New York, the Sahara Desert, and currently with military veterans. She lives in Ithaca, New York.